Silas Barnum Chatfield and His Family: Connecticut, New York, and Wisconsin

Julie K Schellen

Acknowledgement

I would like to thank Karl and Janet Olson, as well as Al Gruling of the East Troy Area Historical Society for answering my numerous questions and providing me with so many wonderful photos, Bible records, publications and personal stories about the Chatfield, Gonia, and Olson families. I would also like to thank my husband, Dr. Mike Schellen, for his never-ending love, patience, and support.

Julie K Schellen, PhD CG®

ISBN: 979-8-9888103-0-8
Library of Congress Control Number: 2023913594

Cover Photo: Chatfield 50th Wedding Anniversary, Troy Center, Wisconsin, 6 May 1907, Silas Barnum and Catherine Kling Chatfield and Family

SILAS BARNUM CHATFIELD AND HIS FAMILY: CONNECTICUT, NEW YORK, AND WISCONSIN

SILAS BARNUM CHATFIELD, the son of Levi and Sarah Runnels Chatfield,[1] was born 21 Oct 1822 in New Milford, Litchfield County, Connecticut.[2] He died 7 Feb 1908 in Troy, Walworth County, Wisconsin[3], and he was buried in Adams Cemetery, Walworth County, Wisconsin.[4] Silas was married to **MARY ELIZABETH HOLCOMB** on 22 Dec 1849 at Palmyra, Wisconsin by the Reverend Eli Carr.[5] Mary was born

Silas Barnum Chatfield
[Courtesy of East Troy Area Historical Society]

© Julie K Schellen, Ph.D., CG®; Dr. Schellen is a college faculty member and professional genealogist and researcher with fifteen years of genealogy research experience. She holds a PhD in Curriculum & Instruction, a Master of Health Services Management, and a BA in Interdisciplinary Studies.

[1] Seneca Chatfield Family Bible, *The Holy Bible* (New York: American Bible Society, 1873); Seneca had possession of his Bible until his death in 1961. In 2001 the Bible was in the possession of Seneca's great niece, Jean A Ralston Ricklefs Agnello, Bellevue, Washington. Jean made photocopies of the Bible pages, and the photocopies are in the possession of the author. The Bible's current location is unknown.

[2] Wisconsin Original Certificate of Death (1908), Silas Barnum Chatfield, Department of Health, Madison.

[3] Alice Chatfield Gonia Family Bible, *The Holy Bible* (Philadelphia, Cincinnati, Chicago & St. Louis: Ziegler & McCurdy, 1872); In 2012 the Bible was in the possession of Alice's granddaughter, Marjorie Jane Ralston Sheets, West Lafayette, Indiana. Marjorie made photocopies of the Bible pages, and the photocopies are in the possession of the author. An inside page reads, "This Holy Bible is willed to Alice Jane Chatfield Gonia by her Father and Mother, 1913." "Silas B Chatfield" appears to be the name engraved on the cover of the Bible. The Bible's current location is unknown.

[4] "Aged Pioneer Passes Away," obituary, *The East Troy News*, Wisconsin, 16 Feb 1908, Silas B Chatfield.

[5] Seneca Chatfield Family Bible, *The Holy Bible* (New York: American Bible Society, 1873).

2 Jan 1831 in New York,[6] and she died 31 Dec 1854.[7] Mary was buried in Adams Cemetery.[8]

Silas was married again on 3 May 1857 to **CATHERINE GASPER KLING** by the Reverend JD Stevens.[9] Catherine, the daughter of Jacob and Dorothy Gasper Kling,[10] was born 10 May 1832 in New Hartford, Oneida County, New York.[11] Catherine died in Troy, Walworth County, Wisconsin on 27 Jul 1915 and was buried in Adams Cemetery.[12]

Biographical Sketch of Silas Barnum Chatfield and Catherine Gasper Kling

After living in New Milford, Connecticut for more than 30 years,[13] Levi Chatfield moved with his family, including his son Silas to Otselic,

---

[6] Seneca Chatfield Family Bible, *The Holy Bible* (New York: American Bible Society, 1873).

[7] *History of Walworth County, Wisconsin.* (Chicago: Western Historical Company, 1882), p. 566. This authored work contains information given to the author by living relatives who had personal knowledge of the people and events.

[8] *Founders Day: The Silas B Chatfield Family.* East Troy Area Historical Society (Troy, Wisconsin, 2018), p. 3.

[9] Wisconsin Marriage Certificate (1857), Silas B Chatfield to Catherine Kling, Department of Health, Madison.

[10] *History of Walworth County, Wisconsin*, 1882, p. 567.

[11] "Catheryn G Chatfield," obituary, *The East Troy News*, Wisconsin, 1 Aug 1915.

[12] Wisconsin Original Certificate of Death (1915), Catherine Gasper Kling Chatfield, Department of Health, Madison.

[13] 1790 U.S. Census, Litchfield County, Connecticut, population schedule, New Milford, p. 71, Levi Chatfield [Sr], database with images, *Ancestry* (www.ancestry.com : accessed 11 June 2023), citing NARA microfilm M637, roll 1; 1800 U.S. Census, Litchfield County, Connecticut, population schedule, New Milford, p. 736, Levi Chatfield [Sr], database with images, *Ancestry* (www.ancestry.com : accessed 5 Aug 2020), citing NARA microfilm M32, roll 52; 1810 U.S. Census, Litchfield County, Connecticut, population schedule, New Milford, p. 140, Levi Chatfield [Jr], database with images, *Ancestry* (www.ancestry.com : accessed 5 Aug 2020), citing NARA microfilm M252, roll 71; 1820 U.S. Census, Litchfield County, Connecticut, population schedule, New Milford, p. 308, Levi Chatfield, Jr, database with images, *Ancestry* (www.ancestry.com : accessed 5 Aug 2020), citing NARA microfilm M33, roll 14.

Chenango County, New York,[14] when Silas was about three years old.[15] Litchfield County, Connecticut, located in the northwest part of the state, was formed in 1751.[16] The main part of Litchfield County is hilly with valleys, and numerous rivers and streams provide water to its residents.[17] By 1836 the county's agricultural interests included raising cattle and sheep, as well as the production of dairy products.[18] The town of New Milford was incorporated in 1712 and originally part of New Haven County.[19] New Milford was mainly a farming community, and by 1830 the population of New Milford included 3,979 residents.[20]

Chenango County, New York, which sits about 200 miles northwest of New Milford, was formed 15 Mar 1798.[21] Chenango County gets its name from the river which flows through it. The county contains beautiful highlands and ridges, which are broken up by charming valleys and steep ravines of the streams situated there.[22] The town of Otselic, Chenango, New York which was settled in 1800 by many settlers migrating from Connecticut and Massachusetts,[23] is located in

---

[14] Albert Clayton Beckwith, *History of Walworth County, Wisconsin* (Indianapolis: B F Bowen & Company, 1912), vol 2, p. 998. This authored work contains information given to the author by living relatives who had personal knowledge of the people and events.

[15] *Founders Day: The Silas B Chatfield Family*, p. 2.

[16] Michael J Leclerc, ed., *Genealogist's Handbook for New England Research*. (Boston, New England Historic Genealogical Society, 2012), p. 33, 75.

[17] *History of Litchfield County, Connecticut with Illustrations and Biographical Sketches of its Prominent Men and Pioneers* (Philadelphia: J W Lewis & Company, 1881) p. 13; digital image, *FamilySearch* (https://www.familysearch.org/library/books/records/item/226207: accessed 5 Aug 2020).

[18] John Warner Barber, *Connecticut Historical Collections, Containing a General Collection… of Every Town in Connecticut* (New Haven, Connecticut: B. L. Hamlen, 1836), p. 452.

[19] Ibid, p. 477.

[20] Ibid, p. 474.

[21] *History of Litchfield County, Connecticut with Illustrations and Biographical Sketches of its Prominent Men and Pioneers*, p. 13.

[22] James H Smith, *History of Chenango and Madison Counties, New York; Some of its Prominent Men and Pioneers* (Syracuse: D Mason & Company, 1880) p. 72; digital image, *Google Books* (https://play.google.com/books/reader?id=9vEpAQAAMAAJ&printsec=frontcover&pg=GBS.PP1: accessed 5 Aug 2020).

[23] *Wikipedia* (http://en.wikipedia.org : accessed 5 Aug 2020), "Otselic, New York."

the northwest corner of the county.[24] Otselic is watered by the river of the same name, and the land was well adapted for the cultivation of grain.[25]

Shortly after Silas' parents moved to New York, Silas' mother Sarah died in Otselic, and his father Levi died there three years later leaving Silas as an orphan.[26] One account indicates that Levi "accidentally suffocated under a haystack and died."[27] If true, Levi had enough time to write a detailed three-page will on 12 January 1833 stating he was "weak in body, but of sound mind," before he died. Levi Chatfield's half-brother David Bard appeared in court on 18 February 1833 as executor of the estate.[28]

Silas' uncle, David Bard became his guardian,[29] and Silas was soon bound out to a farmer named Theodore Burchard in nearby Hamilton, Madison County, New York.[30] Later, when Mr. Burchard rented his farm out to James Stratton, Silas continued to live on the farm with Mr. Stratton until Silas was eighteen years old.[31] By all accounts, Silas enjoyed living with Mr. and Mrs. Stratton, as much as they enjoyed him living with them.[32] Once Silas became an adult, he was given two suits of clothes, a Bible and one hundred dollars.[33] His Bible would serve as

---

[24] *New York Family History Research Guide and Gazetteer.* (New York: New York Genealogical and Biographical Society, 2017), p. 339, 342.

[25] James H Smith, *History of Chenango and Madison Counties, New York; Some of its Prominent Men and Pioneers,* p. 73.

[26] "Aged Pioneer Passes Away," obituary, Silas B Chatfield.

[27] *Founders Day: The Silas B Chatfield Family,* p. 2.

[28] Chenango County, New York, Probate Court, Chenango County Clerk, "New York, Wills and Probate records, 1659-1999," *Ancestry* (https://www.ancestry.com/imageviewer/collections/8800/images/005115219_00 100?pId=1976332 : accessed 11 Jun 2023), Chenango > Wills, Vol. C-D, 1830-1840, digital images, image 100 of 405, volume C, pp. 143-148, Levi Chatfield, signed 12 January 1833, recorded 18 Feb 1833, proved 18 July 1833.

[29] Ibid.

[30] "Aged Pioneer Passes Away," obituary, Silas B Chatfield.

[31] *History of Walworth County, Wisconsin,* 1882, p. 566.

[32] John B Cameron, *Souvenir of the 50th Wedding Anniversary of Silas B. Chatfield and Catherine Chatfield, 1857-1907,* (Troy, Wisconsin: Privately Printed, 1907).

[33] "Aged Pioneer Passes Away," obituary, Silas B Chatfield.

his guide for the rest of his life,[34] and in Hamilton he joined the Baptist Church.[35] Silas then attended school for a term and worked as a laborer.[36] After a few years, he headed west. He worked various jobs along the way, stopped to visit his uncle who was living in Ohio by that time, and made his way to Troy, Walworth County, Wisconsin where his friend James Stratton had moved in 1843.[37]

For decades, pioneers pushed further westward towards the Frontier line, and at the close of the War of 1812, there was a significant increase in the number of settlers moving west over the United States.[38] By the 1830s and 1840s, people flooded west towards a number of territories, and one of those territories was Wisconsin.[39] The Territory of Wisconsin was created on 20 Apr 1836 by an act of the United States Congress.[40] By the end of that year farmers from New England and New York began settling in the lush prairie groves in the counties surrounding Milwaukee, Wisconsin.[41] Many of these early settlers arrived with few possessions, made many of their own tools, and cleared wooded land to build their homes and plant crops.[42] Settlers faced difficult travel on old Indian trails that were only about fifteen inches wide and resembled ditches more than they resembled roads.[43]

Walworth County, Wisconsin is in the southeast corner of the state, and the town of Troy is in the northeastern portion of Walworth County. Troy is home to beautiful prairie lands, groves of trees, two creeks and several small lakes.[44] Troy also contains about 3,000 acres

---

[34] *Founders Day: The Silas B Chatfield Family*, p. 2.
[35] John B Cameron, *Souvenir of the 50th Wedding Anniversary of Silas B. Chatfield and Catherine Chatfield, 1857-1907*.
[36] *History of Walworth County, Wisconsin*, 1882, p. 566.
[37] *Founders Day: The Silas B Chatfield Family*, p. 2.
[38] *Britannica* (https://www.britannica.com : accessed 5 Aug 2020), "Westward Movement: United States History."
[39] Ibid.
[40] *Wikipedia* (http://en.wikipedia.org : accessed 3 Aug 2020), "History of Wisconsin."
[41] Ibid.
[42] Seneca B Chatfield, *History of the Adams Community* (Troy, Wisconsin: East Troy Area Historical Society, 1952). Seneca was the son of Silas B Chatfield.
[43] Albert Clayton Beckwith, *History of Walworth County, Wisconsin*, vol 1, p. 183.
[44] *History of Walworth County, Wisconsin*, 1882, p. 552.

of wetland.[45] Honey Creek, which runs through the town, was named by the early settlers, because of the numerous honeybees that lived in the trees along its banks.[46] Originally, Troy Township was made up of five unincorporated communities: Troy, Troy Center, Adams, Mayhew, and Little Prairie.[47] The Mayhew community is now a ghost town.[48]

Silas arrived in Troy on 1 Nov 1846 with $301.00 in his pocket.[49] Less than a year after his arrival, Silas purchased eighty acres in Troy from James Stratton for $500.00 on 14 Jun 1847.[50] A few months later, Silas purchased forty acres in Troy from Asa Bartlett for $70.00 on 10 Dec 1847.[51] This land, located in the Adams community, would later become the Chatfield Family Farm where he would live for the rest of his life.[52] Once he purchased the land, he cleared it and began building a nice and comfortable home.[53] Once he completed the home, he asked for Mary Elizabeth Holcomb's hand in marriage,[54] and on 22 Dec 1849

---

[45] Al Gruling, "Town of Troy History," *Town of Troy* (https://townoftroy.com/town-history/ : accessed 28 Jul 2020).

[46] Ibid.

[47] Ibid.

[48] *Wikipedia* (http://en.wikipedia.org : accessed 18 Aug 2020), "Mayhews, Wisconsin."

[49] *Founders Day: The Silas B Chatfield Family*, p. 2.

[50] *FamilySearch* (https://www.familysearch.org/ark:/61903/3:1:3Q9M-CSL2-HS1Q-8?i=249&cat=571568 : accessed 11 Jun 2023, digital film 8197660, images 250-1 of 794, "Deeds, 1839-1921; Indexes 1839-1901," Troy, Walworth County, Wisconsin, Register of Deeds, vol. 8, p. 17-18, signed 14 Jun 1847, recorded 5 Oct 1847, James Stratton of Troy to Silas B Chatfield of Troy.

[51] *FamilySearch* (https://www.familysearch.org/ark:/61903/3:1:3Q9M-CSL2-F9FK-S?i=391&cat=571568 : accessed 11 Jun 2023), digital film 8197911, images 392-3 of 796, "Deeds, 1839-1921; Indexes 1839-1901," Troy, Walworth County, Wisconsin, Register of Deeds, vol. 32, p. 493-4, Asa Bartlett to Silas Chatfield, signed 10 Dec 1847, recorded 10 Sep 1862.

[52] Albert Clayton Beckwith, *History of Walworth County, Wisconsin*, vol 2, p. 998.

[53] Ibid.

[54] Ibid.

they married.[55] Silas became a successful farmer fairly quickly, and by 1850, the value of Silas Chatfield's real estate had increased to $1,000.[56]

Silas' early success as a farmer would soon be followed by tragedy, when his wife Mary died after she slipped and fell on the doorstep of their home on 31 Dec 1854.[57] Silas's two small boys would lose their mother, as he did as a small boy back in New York. Mary was buried on a portion of the farm that would later become Adams Cemetery.[58] Another resident, Mrs. Porter who had died the previous year and was buried at her family's farm was reinterred at Adams Cemetery as well.[59] On 22 Sep 1855, Silas sold the land, which totaled 51 hundredths of an acre to the Adams Cemetery Association for the sum of $1.00.[60]

Silas raised two young sons alone for several years until he met and then married Catherine Gasper Kling on 3 May 1857.[61] Catherine, the youngest child of Jacob and Dorothy Gasper Kling,[62] was born on 10 May 1832 in New Hartford, Oneida County, New York.[63] Her parents, Jacob and Dorothy Kling were both born in Sharon, Schoharie County, New York and relocated to Yorkville, Oneida County, New

---

[55] Seneca Chatfield Family Bible, 1873.

[56] 1850 U.S. Census, Walworth County, Wisconsin, population schedule, Troy, p. 228A, Silas Chatfield; database with images, *Ancestry* (www.ancestry.com : accessed 28 Jul 2020); citing NARA microfilm M432.

[57] *Founders Day: The Silas B Chatfield Family*, p. 3.

[58] Ibid.

[59] Ibid.

[60] *FamilySearch* (https://www.familysearch.org/ark:/61903/3:1:3Q9M-CSL2-CQNY?i=758&cat=571568 : accessed 11 Jun 2023), digital film 8197909, images 759 of 795, "Deeds, 1839-1921; Indexes 1839-1901," Troy, Walworth County, Wisconsin, Register of Deeds, vol. 48, p. 107, Silas B Chatfield of Troy to Adams Cemetery Association of Troy, signed 22 Sep 1855, recorded 23 Feb 1870.

[61] Wisconsin Marriage Certificate (1857), Silas B Chatfield to Catherine Kling, Department of Health, Madison.

[62] Wisconsin Original Certificate of Death (1915), Catherine Gasper Kling Chatfield, Department of Health, Madison.

[63] "Catheryn G Chatfield," obituary, *The East Troy News*, Wisconsin, 1 Aug 1915.

York in 1835 a few years after Catherine was born.[64] Yorkville, which is now a part of Utica, was a bustling city at the time due to the newly completed Erie Canal.[65] The opening of the Erie Canal had a tremendous economic impact not just on the communities along the waterway, but on the state of New York and the surrounding areas in general by lowering the cost of transportation, and easing the ability of merchants to ship goods to the Midwest and Northwest.[66] Jacob earned his living there as a shoemaker, an occupation that would follow him the rest of his life.[67] Catherine attended school in New York until she was thirteen years old, and she would often visit the local cotton factory where her sister worked.[68] Catherine would watch the workers for hours, learned how to weave and eventually began working at the factory alongside her sister.[69]

In the 1840s, when many New York settlers began migrating westward to the newly opened state of Wisconsin,[70] Jacob and Dorothy Kling and their younger children set off for Troy.[71] The Kling family arrived in Troy in May 1849, and Catherine eventually attended Milton College for a term and began teaching at the Lauderdale Lakes School.[72] She worked as a teacher for the next five years until she married Silas.[73] Jacob and Dorothy remained in Wisconsin and spent the rest of their

---

[64] Margaret E Kling, *Genealogical History of John Ludwig Kling and his Descendants, 1755-1924* (Amsterdam, New York : Higginson Book Company, 1924) p. 28; digital image, *Google Books* (https://www.google.com : accessed 10 Aug 2020). Margaret E Kling's father and Catherine Kling Chatfield were first cousins.

[65] *The Erie Canal* (http://eriecanal.org/history.html), "History of the Erie Canal," accessed 10 Aug 2020.

[66] *Wikipedia* (http://en.wikipedia.org : accessed 10 Aug 2020), "Erie Canal."

[67] Margaret E Kling, *Genealogical History of John Ludwig Kling and his Descendants, 1755-1924*, p. 28.

[68] "Catheryn G Chatfield," obituary.

[69] Ibid.

[70] *Encyclopedia Britannica* (https://www.britannica.com : accessed 5 Aug 2020), "Westward Movement: United States History."

[71] Margaret E Kling, *Genealogical History of John Ludwig Kling and his Descendants, 1755-1924*, p. 28.

[72] "Catheryn G Chatfield," obituary.

[73] Margaret E Kling, *Genealogical History of John Ludwig Kling and his Descendants, 1755-1924*, p. 28.

lives in Troy.[74] In 1882, Catherine's father, Jacob Kling, who was 97 years old, was the oldest living man in Walworth County, Wisconsin.[75]

| Name | Age | Occupation | Value | | Birthplace |
			Real estate	Personal estate	
Silas Chatfield	37	Farmer	3,125	650	Connecticut
Catherine Chatfield	27				New York
Norman Chatfield	9				Wisconsin
Levi Chatfield	7				Wisconsin
George Chatfield	1				Wisconsin
Omar Chatfield	1/12				Wisconsin
Peter Niland	18	Farm Laborer			Ireland
Frances Holcomb	27	Domestic			New York

Table 1
Silas Chatfield Household in the 1860 U.S. Census[a]
Troy, Walworth County, Wisconsin

a. 1860 U.S. Census, Walworth County, Wisconsin, population schedule, Troy, p. 610, Silas Chatfield; database with images, *Ancestry* (www.ancestry.com : accessed 28 Jul 2020); citing NARA microfilm M653.

Silas prospered as a farmer, and some of the first crops of early settlers in Troy included grain and wheat.[76] Forty years later, agricultural grasses were still one of the main crops produced in Walworth County.[77] The Chatfield farm eventually produced sugar cane, and Silas manufactured cane syrup for almost fifteen years.[78] In addition, a gravel pit located on Silas' land provided gravel for some of the roads near his farm.[79] By 1860, Silas had increased the value of his real and personal estate to almost $3800.00 allowing him to hire additional farm and domestic help.[80]

---

[74] "Catheryn G Chatfield," obituary, *The East Troy News*, Wisconsin, 1 Aug 1915.
[75] *History of Walworth County, Wisconsin*, 1882, p. 567.
[76] Ibid, p. 561.
[77] Ibid, p. 261.
[78] Seneca B Chatfield, *History of the Adams Community*, 1952.
[79] Ibid.
[80] 1860 U.S. Census, Walworth County, Wisconsin, population schedule, Troy, p. 610, Silas Chatfield; database with images, *Ancestry* (www.ancestry.com : accessed 28 Jul 2020); citing NARA microfilm M653.

In 1862, Silas' wife Catherine offered to assist a neighbor deliver a baby, and this experience set her up as a midwife who regularly helped deliver babies for other neighbors for much of her life.[81] Midwives in the nineteenth century, were generally local women who were mothers themselves.[82] These local women gained experience by attending the births of friends and neighbors, likely as an apprentice at first by watching and assisting in the birth.[83] Midwives were important in the communities, as childbirth during this time was difficult and often a dangerous experience for the woman.[84] Catherine's long career as a midwife in Troy allowed her to deliver one hundred and eight babies in thirty-eight years, including many of her own grandchildren.[85] Mrs. Chatfield was always willing to offer her services to help the sick and those in need, and she was known by her friends and family as Aunt Kate or Grandma Chatfield.[86]

In 1863, the federal government began the necessary task of enrolling and drafting men into the Civil War.[87] Silas can be found in the U S Civil War Consolidated Enrollment list for Class II persons in Troy, Walworth County, Wisconsin, dated 30 Jun 1863.[88] The Class II list for the First Congressional District, the district in which Walworth County sat, included married men ages 36-44.[89] However, no further records

---

[81] *Founders Day: The Silas B Chatfield Family*, p. 3.
[82] *Britannica* (https://www.britannica.com : accessed 15 Aug 2020), "Midwifery."
[83] Ibid.
[84] *Midwives in 19th Century America* (https://www.womenhistoryblog.com : accessed 15 Aug 2020).
[85] "Midwife Helped Deliver Over 100 Babies Here!" *The East Troy News*, Wisconsin, 18 Mar 1970. The list published is taken from Catherine Chatfield's old medical delivery record book, in which she recorded the names of the mothers, the dates, the sex of the baby, the health of the baby at the time of delivery, and occasionally the baby's weight.
[86] "Catheryn G Chatfield," obituary, *The East Troy News*, Wisconsin, 1 Aug 1915.
[87] *FamilySearch Wiki* (https://www.familysearch.org/wiki : accessed 14 Aug 2020), "Union Draft Records."
[88] U.S., Civil War Draft Registrations Records, 1863-1865; database with images, *Ancestry* (www.ancestry.com : accessed 14 Aug 2020); citing NARA, Consolidated Enrollment Lists, 1863-1865, record group 110.
[89] *FamilySearch Wiki* (https://www.familysearch.org/wiki : accessed 14 Aug 2020), "Union Draft Records."

could be found that indicated Silas participated in the war beyond the 1863 enrollment list. Silas' son Seneca, who wrote several biographies and newspaper articles about his father, including Silas' obituary, also never mentioned any Civil War involvement in any of them.

Still experiencing success as a farmer, Silas had increased the value of his real and personal estate to over $4600.00 by 1870.[90] His two oldest sons were old enough now to help their father as laborers on the family farm.[91] Silas Chatfield was manufacturing sorghum on his farm and attended the Sugar Cane Grower's and Manufacturer's Convention in Palmyra, Wisconsin in 1879 to exhibit two samples of his mush cane sugar and syrup.[92] By 1882, Silas maintained one of the busiest sorghum mills in the area,[93] and by September 1888 both day and night workers were employed at the mill.[94] Farmers would bring wagonloads of cane, so that the juice could be squeezed out of the cane.[95] Cooking of the juice created a heavy dark sorghum syrup similar to molasses.[96] In October 1897, the mill caught fire, and Silas lost about $1,000 in contents.[97] The Chatfield family recovered from that loss and operated

---

[90] 1870 U.S. Census, Walworth County, Wisconsin, population schedule, Troy, p. 263, Silas Chatfield; database with images, *Ancestry* (www.ancestry.com : accessed 28 Jul 2020); citing NARA microfilm M593.

[91] Ibid.

[92] "Sugar Cane Grower's and Manufacturer's Convention," *The Whitewater Register* (Whitewater, Wisconsin), 6 Mar 1879, p. 2, digital image, *Irvin L. Young Memorial Library Community History Archive* (http://irvinlyoung.advantage-preservation.com/ : accessed 2 Sep 2020).

[93] "Sorghum Manufacturers," *The Whitewater Register* (Whitewater, Wisconsin), 23 Nov 1882, p. 2, digital image, *Irvin L. Young Memorial Library Community History Archive* (http://irvinlyoung.advantage-preservation.com/ : accessed 31 Aug 2020).

[94] "S. B. Chatfield and Son," *The Whitewater Register* (Whitewater, Wisconsin), 27 Sep 1888, p. 1, digital image, *Irvin L. Young Memorial Library Community History Archive* (http://irvinlyoung.advantage-preservation.com/ : accessed 31 Aug 2020).

[95] Seneca B Chatfield, *History of the Adams Community*, 1952.

[96] Ibid.

[97] "The S. B. Chatfield Sorghum Factory," *The Whitewater Register* (Whitewater, Wisconsin), 21 Oct 1897, p. 3, digital image, *Irvin L. Young Memorial Library Community History Archive* (http://irvinlyoung.advantage-preservation.com/ : accessed 31 Aug 2020).

the sorghum mill until it was finally destroyed by a tornado on 22 Apr 1914 and never rebuilt.[98]

| Name | Age | Occupation | Value | | Birthplace |
			Real estate	Personal estate	
Silas B Chatfield	47	Farmer	3,500	1,120	Connecticut
Catherine Chatfield	38	Keeping House			New York
Norman A Chatfield	19	Farmer			Wisconsin
Levi Chatfield	17	Farm Laborer			Wisconsin
George Chatfield	11	At home			Wisconsin
Omer Chatfield	10	At home			Wisconsin
DeWitt Chatfield	7				Wisconsin
Jane Chatfield	6				Wisconsin
Libbie Chatfield	10/12				Wisconsin

Table 2

Silas Chatfield Household in the 1870 U.S. Census[a]

Troy, Walworth County, Wisconsin

a. 1870 U.S. Census, Walworth County, Wisconsin, population schedule, Troy, p. 263, Silas Chatfield; database with images, *Ancestry* (www.ancestry.com : accessed 28 Jul 2020); citing NARA microfilm M593.

In 1877, Silas set about building a much larger home on the farm to accommodate his growing family of nine children.[99]   Silas, who had knowledge of stone masonry, had been gradually making his house plans, and by May 1879, he was laying much of the foundation himself.[100] By October, his new house was approaching completion with the exterior finished to imitate the look of sandstone.[101] The larger

---

[98] *Founders Day: The Silas B Chatfield Family*, p. 3.
[99] Ibid.
[100] "Mr. Silas Chatfield of Adams," *The Whitewater Register* (Whitewater, Wisconsin), 8 May 1879, p. 3, digital image, *Irvin L. Young Memorial Library Community History Archive* (http://irvinlyoung.advantage-preservation.com/ : accessed 31 Aug 2020).
[101] "Silas Chatfield of Adams is Busy," *The Whitewater Register* (Whitewater, Wisconsin), 9 Oct 1879, p. 3, digital image, *Irvin L. Young Memorial Library Community History Archive* (http://irvinlyoung.advantage-preservation.com/ : accessed 31 Aug 2020).

house took some time to complete, but it eventually included fourteen rooms and provided his family with much needed space.[102]

Catherine Chatfield, who was college educated and worked previously as a teacher was likely influential in the education of her own children.[103] All of the Chatfield children learned to read and write, and when the Chatfield children were school-aged, they attended school.[104] An interest in teaching was also passed on to Silas and Catherine's children, as Sarah Elizabeth taught school in Downers Grove, Illinois for several years,[105] and Seneca taught school for a year after he graduated East Troy High School in 1900.[106] He then worked as a bookkeeper for the *American School Board Journal* for a year before returning to farming after his father, Silas died.[107] Seneca served as the Town Clerk for twenty-five years.[108]

A new schoolhouse was built in the Adams community in 1881, and once the building was finished, Silas Chatfield and his neighbor Hirand Nourse organized the Adams Methodist Episcopal Church.[109] Prior to the use of the schoolhouse, residents either traveled to neighboring communities to attend church or services were held in local homes.[110]

---

[102] *Founders Day: The Silas B Chatfield Family*, p. 3.

[103] "Catheryn G Chatfield," obituary.

[104] 1860 U.S. Census, Walworth County, Wisconsin, population schedule, Troy, p. 610, Silas Chatfield; database with images, *Ancestry* (www.ancestry.com : accessed 28 Jul 2020); citing NARA microfilm M653; 1870 U.S. Census, Walworth County, Wisconsin, population schedule, Troy, p. 263, Silas Chatfield; database with images, *Ancestry* (www.ancestry.com : accessed 28 Jul 2020); citing NARA microfilm M593; 1880 U.S. Census, Walworth County, Wisconsin, population schedule, Troy, p. 225B, Enumeration District 236, Silas B Chatfield; database with images, Ancestry (www.ancestry.com : accessed 18 Aug 2020).

[105] "Elizabeth Chatfield Escher," obituary, *The Whitewater Register* (Whitewater, Wisconsin), 12 Dec 1901, p. 8, digital image, *Irvin L. Young Memorial Library Community History Archive* (http://irvinlyoung.advantage-preservation.com/ : accessed 31 Aug 2020).

[106] *Founders Day: The Silas B Chatfield Family*, p. 6.

[107] Albert Clayton Beckwith, *History of Walworth County, Wisconsin,* vol 2, p. 998.

[108] *Founders Day: The Silas B Chatfield Family*, p. 6.

[109] Al Gruling, "Town of Troy History," *Town of Troy.*

[110] *Founders Day: The Silas B Chatfield Family*, p. 3.

Some settlers traveled a great distance to attend church.[111] Silas, a religious man since the age of eighteen, enjoyed being active in Sunday School.[112] He was an early fundraiser for the church and would host successful community socials at his house, in which ice cream and cake would be served, and the proceeds of the party would be used to purchase supplies for the Sunday School at the Adams schoolhouse.[113] Silas attended church regularly until his health made it impossible to attend later in life.[114]

When the first pioneers settled in Walworth County, access to mail facilities was limited.[115] In 1836, the closest post office was in Racine, and all mail arriving and departing Walworth County had to pass through Racine, thus greatly delaying the pickup and delivery of mail to the area.[116] By the 1850s more and more communities housed local post offices, and the process for sending and receiving mail greatly improved.[117] Silas was appointed the Postmaster of the Adams Post Office on 9 Aug 1850,[118] and almost thirty-eight years later, his wife, Catherine was appointed the Postmaster of the Adams Post Office on 28 Apr 1888.[119] Silas and Catherine's son DeWitt was appointed the Adams mail carrier when Catherine took over as Postmaster.[120]

The Adams Post Office, which moved to the Chatfield home while Catherine was Postmaster, maintained twenty-four mailboxes, and the

---

[111] Seneca B Chatfield, *History of the Adams Community*, 1952.

[112] "Aged Pioneer Passes Away," obituary, Silas B Chatfield.

[113] "The Blue Jay Sociable," *The Whitewater Register* (Whitewater, Wisconsin), 30 Jul 1891, *Irvin L. Young Memorial Library Community History Archive* (http://irvinlyoung.advantage-preservation.com/ : accessed 31 Aug 2020).

[114] "Aged Pioneer Passes Away," obituary, Silas B Chatfield.

[115] *History of Walworth County, Wisconsin*. p. 331.

[116] *History of Walworth County, Wisconsin*. p. 331.

[117] "U. S. Postmasters, 1832-1911," database with images, *Ancestry* (https://www.ancestry.com : accessed 19 Aug 2020), pp. 244-245, Walworth County; list of local post offices between 1849 and 1854.

[118] "U. S. Postmasters, 1832-1911," pp. 244-245, Walworth County, Silas B Chatfield, appointed 9 Aug 1850.

[119] "U. S. Postmasters, 1832-1911," pp. 454-455, Walworth County, Catherine Chatfield, appointed 28 Apr 1888.

[120] Seneca B Chatfield, *History of the Adams Community*, 1952.

mail was kept in the individual mailboxes until residents could stop by to pick up their mail.[121] The Chatfield children were instructed by their parents not to touch the mail in the mailboxes or Uncle Sam would come and get them.[122] Catherine contributed news items to the Elkhorn newspaper for almost thirty years about the families who lived within the Adams Post Office delivery area.[123] The Adams Post Office remained in the Chatfield home until the government closed the Adams location on 15 Sep 1903, and the Eagle Post Office took over the mail for the Adams community.[124]

Silas Chatfield and other area farmers organized a cooperative venture and built the Adams creamery in 1893, which was located across the road from the Chatfield farm.[125] A man from Whitewater, Wisconsin named Harvey Marr provided the cheese making equipment, and both cheese and butter were produced at the creamery until it closed in 1917.[126] Dairy farmers would travel for miles to bring wagons and horses loaded with cans of milk, so the milk could be converted to cheese and butter.[127] During the summer months the residents would gather to make various flavors of ice cream, and the children eagerly volunteered to clean the ice cream off the ladles.[128]

Silas and Catherine Chatfield enjoyed an active social life. A few newspaper excerpts include:

- ...on last Saturday evening the 6th... was celebrated the silver wedding of S. B. Chatfield and wife and about one hundred ladies, gentlemen and children responded to their

---

[121] Seneca B Chatfield, *History of the Adams Community*, 1952.

[122] Ibid.

[123] Albert Clayton Beckwith, *History of Walworth County, Wisconsin*, vol 1, p. 499.

[124] "U. S. Postmasters, 1832-1911," pp. 454-455, Walworth County.

[125] *Founders Day: The Silas B Chatfield Family*, p. 3.

[126] Seneca B Chatfield, *History of the Adams Community*, 1952.

[127] Hoard Historical Museum, *Creameries* (https://hoardmuseum.org : accessed 19 Aug 2020).

[128] Seneca B Chatfield, *History of the Adams Community*, 1952.

invitations…Mirth and good humor held the party until nearly midnight when they retired to their homes…[129]

- Mrs. S. B. Chatfield and Miss Clara Nourse drove to William Tess' at Honey Creek, on Saturday remaining over the Sabbath.[130]

- Mr. and Mrs. S. B. Chatfield gave an entertainment to Mr. and Mrs. O. C. Chatfield, of South Superior, last Thursday evening, it being their twelfth wedding anniversary.[131]

- Mrs. Pember and Miss Cook of Vernon, were callers on Mrs. S. B. Chatfield last Thursday while on their way to Heart Prairie…[132]

- Twelve of the ladies in this neighborhood made it pleasant last Saturday at the home of Mrs. S. B. Chatfield. In the event of Sunday being her 71st birthday. They surprised her on Saturday afternoon.[133]

- A Chatfield "brunch" consisting of Mr. and Mrs. Levi Chatfield, Mr. and Mrs. Levi Gonia (nee Chatfield) with Kittie and Maud Gonia of Adams…enjoyed the hospitality of Mr. and Mrs. S. B. Chatfield from Thursday evening to Sunday evening.[134]

---

[129] "On Last Saturday Evening," *The Whitewater Register* (Whitewater, Wisconsin), 11 May 1882, p. 3, digital image, *Irvin L. Young Memorial Library Community History Archive* (http://irvinlyoung.advantage-preservation.com/ : accessed 2 Sep 2020).

[130] "Adams," *The Whitewater Register* (Whitewater, Wisconsin), 15 Oct 1891, p. 8, digital image, *Irvin L. Young Memorial Library Community History Archive* (http://irvinlyoung.advantage-preservation.com/ : accessed 2 Sep 2020).

[131] "Twelfth Wedding Anniversary," *The Whitewater Register* (Whitewater, Wisconsin), 4 May 1893, p. 8, digital image, *Irvin L. Young Memorial Library Community History Archive* (http://irvinlyoung.advantage-preservation.com/ : accessed 2 Sep 2020).

[132] "Mrs. Pember and Miss Cook," *The Whitewater Register* (Whitewater, Wisconsin), 19 Oct 1893, p. 8, digital image, *Irvin L. Young Memorial Library Community History Archive* (http://irvinlyoung.advantage-preservation.com/ : accessed 2 Sep 2020).

[133] "71st Birthday," *The Whitewater Register* (Whitewater, Wisconsin), 14 May 1903, p. 8, digital image, *Irvin L. Young Memorial Library Community History Archive* (http://young.advantage-preservation.com/ : accessed 2 Sep 2020).

[134] "A Chatfield Brunch," *The Whitewater Register* (Whitewater, Wisconsin), 31 Dec 1903, p. 8, digital image, *Irvin L. Young Memorial Library Community History Archive* (http://irvinlyoung.advantage-preservation.com/ : accessed 2 Sep 2020).

Chatfield Farm- 1953
[Courtesy of East Troy Area Historical Society]

Silas wrote his will in Troy on 13 Sep 1902 naming his wife and all surviving children, and on 20 Jan 1908, he added a codicil to it naming the children of his deceased son Norman, removing George who had received his share of the inheritance before 1908, and mentioning Alice who had been paid her share prior to 1902.[135] Silas died 7 Feb 1908.[136]

Silas' son Seneca was appointed executor of his estate, and after Silas' widow Catherine died on 27 Jul 1915, the remainder of the estate was distributed to the heirs.[137] Silas and Catherine's son Seneca lived on the Chatfield farm until his death in 1961, and the property was eventually

---

[135] Walworth County, Wisconsin, Register in Probate, Will and Probate Record, Silas B. Chatfield, No. 7402, vol. 5, p. 441, vol. 28, p. 517, vol. 71, p. 373 and vol. 81, p. 38, 94, will recorded 17 Mar 1908, Walworth County, Wisconsin, Courthouse, Elkhorn.

[136] Wisconsin Original Certificate of Death (1908), Silas Barnum Chatfield, Department of Health, Madison; "Aged Pioneer Passes Away," obituary, Silas B Chatfield.

[137] Walworth County, Wisconsin, Register in Probate, Will and Probate Record, Silas B. Chatfield, No. 7402, vol. 81, p. 38, 94, Final Judgment, 20 Dec 1915, Walworth County, Wisconsin, Courthouse, Elkhorn.

sold out of the family after Seneca's wife Ella died in 1970.[138] The farmhouse that Silas Chatfield built in 1879 still stands today.[139]

Silas Barnum Chatfield and his first wife Mary Elizabeth Holcomb had two known children:

    i.   NORMAN ALONZO CHATFIELD was born 6 Nov 1850 in Troy, Walworth County, Wisconsin.[140] He was married to Lillian E Allen on 15 Nov 1871 at Charles City, Iowa by Reverend C Manwell.[141] Lillian was born 14 Mar 1854 in Russell, Ontario, Canada and died 18 Jul 1934 in Waterloo, Black Hawk County, Iowa.[142] Lillian was buried in Adams Cemetery.[143] Norman died 26 Jun 1894 in Troy,[144] and he was buried in Adams Cemetery.[145]

    ii.   LEVI LEROY CHATFIELD was born 5 Jul 1852 in Troy.[146] Levi was married to Bertha Rhodes on 25 Feb 1903 at Troy

---

[138] Walworth County, Wisconsin, Deed Records, vol. 156, p. 311, No. 223586, Irene C Norton [Estate of Catherine Chatfield] to Seneca B. Chatfield, and Ella M. Chatfield, his wife, recorded 5 Dec 1919; Walworth County, Wisconsin, Deed Records, vol. 564, p. 375, No. 528702, Estate of Seneca Chatfield to Ella Chatfield, Troy, recorded 2 May 1961; and Walworth County, Wisconsin, Deed Records, vol. 33, p. 77, No. 627439, Estate of Ella Chatfield to Ervin J and Elsie B. Dominski, Troy, recorded 14 Aug 1970, Walworth County, Wisconsin, Courthouse, Elkhorn.

[139] [(PRIVATE)], East Troy Area Historical Society, Wisconsin [(E-ADDRESS FOR PRIVATE USE),] to Julie Schellen, e-mail, 29 August 2020, "Chatfield Farmhouse," Personal Correspondence Folder, Chatfield Research Files; privately held by Schellen [(E-ADDRESS), & STREET ADDRESS FOR PRIVATE USE], Colleyville, Texas, 2020. [(PRIVATE)], personally knew Kathryn Gonia Olson and attended the estate sale.

[140] Alice Chatfield Gonia Family Bible, 1872.

[141] Seneca Chatfield Family Bible, 1873.

[142] Iowa, Standard Certificate of Death (1934), Lillian Clayton, Iowa State Department of Health, Des Moines.

[143] *Find A Grave*. Database with images. (http://www.findagrave.com : accessed 15 Aug 2020), memorial 110641376, Lillian Clayton (1854-1934), Adams Cemetery, Troy, Walworth County, Wisconsin; gravestone photograph by LKopet.

[144] "Norman Alonzo Chatfield," obituary, *The East Troy News*, Wisconsin, 24 Jun 1894.

[145] *Find A Grave*. Database with images. (http://www.findagrave.com : accessed 7 Aug 2020), memorial 114919690, Norman A Chatfield (1850-1894), Adams Cemetery, Troy, Walworth County, Wisconsin; gravestone photograph by PPatton.

[146] Alice Chatfield Gonia Family Bible, 1872.

Center, Walworth County, Wisconsin by Reverend J McLain.[147] Bertha was born 7 Aug 1871 in Kansas, and she died 29 Sep 1953 in Crown Point, Lake County, Indiana.[148] She was buried in Maplewood Cemetery in Crown Point.[149] Levi died 1 May 1917 in Crown Point.[150] Levi was buried in Maplewood Cemetery.[151]

Silas Barnum Chatfield and his second wife Catherine Gasper Kling had seven known children:

 iii. GEORGE KLING CHATFIELD was born 8 Jun 1858 in Troy.[152] He was married to Manetta McCarthy on 21 Dec 1881 in Eagle Township by Reverend George Haycroft.[153] Manetta was born 3 Jun 1863 in Eagle, Waukesha, Wisconsin and died 31 July 1947[154] in Janesville, Rock County, Wisconsin.[155] She was buried in Milton Junction Cemetery.[156] George died 29 April 1925 in Milton Junction,

---

[147] Seneca Chatfield Family Bible, 1873.

[148] Indiana Certificate of Death (1953), Bertha Chatfield; Indiana State Board of Health, Indianapolis.

[149] *Find A Grave*. Database with images. (http://www.findagrave.com : accessed 15 Aug 2020), memorial 97069737, Bertha L Chatfield (1871-1953), Maplewood Cemetery, Crown Point, Lake County, Indiana; gravestone photograph by IBill.

[150] Indiana Certificate of Death (1917), Levi Leroy Chatfield; Indiana State Board of Health, Indianapolis.

[151] *Find A Grave*. Database with images. (http://www.findagrave.com : accessed 7 Aug 2020), memorial 97069727, Levi Leroy L Chatfield (1852-1917), Maplewood Cemetery, Crown Point, Lake County, Indiana; gravestone photograph by IBill.

[152] Alice Chatfield Gonia Family Bible, 1872.

[153] Seneca Chatfield Family Bible, 1873.

[154] "Mrs. Manetta F Chatfield," obituary, *The Capital Times*, Wisconsin, 3 Aug 1974, p. 12, *Newspapers* (https://www.newspapers.com : accessed 7 Aug 2020).

[155] *Find A Grave*. Database with images. (http://www.findagrave.com : accessed 15 Aug 2020), memorial 9394255, M. F. Chatfield (1863-1947), Milton Junction Cemetery, Milton Junction, Rock County, Wisconsin; gravestone photograph by MSeeker.

[156] Ibid.

Rock County, Wisconsin,[157] and he was buried in Milton Junction Cemetery.[158]

iv. OMER CORNING CHATFIELD was born 24 Apr 1860 in Troy.[159] He was married to Isabelle Lackey on 27 Apr 1881 by Reverend George Haycroft.[160] Isabelle was born 8 Apr 1860 in Delavan, Walworth County, Wisconsin and died 8 Jan 1943[161] in West Allis, Milwaukee County, Wisconsin.[162] She is buried in Adams Cemetery.[163] Omer died 20 Jun 1908 in West Allis, Milwaukee County, Wisconsin, and he was buried in Troy.[164]

v. DEWITT CLINTON CHATFIELD was born 11 Aug 1862 in Troy.[165] He was married to Makie Elizabeth Rhodes on 27 Aug 1884 by Reverend H Connor.[166] Makie was born 21 Oct 1866 in Crown Point, Indiana,[167] and she died 17 Jan

---

[157] Wisconsin Original Certificate of Death (1925), George Kling Chatfield, Department of Health, Madison.

[158] *Find A Grave.* Database with images. (http://www.findagrave.com : accessed 7 Aug 2020), memorial 9394257, George Kling Chatfield (1858-1925), Milton Junction Cemetery, Milton Junction, Rock County, Wisconsin; gravestone photograph by AGruling.

[159] Alice Chatfield Gonia Family Bible, 1872.

[160] Seneca Chatfield Family Bible, 1873.

[161] "Chatfield: Belle Lackey," obituary, *Milwaukee Sentinel*, Tue, 12 Jan 1943, p. 16.

[162] *Find A Grave.* Database with images. (http://www.findagrave.com : accessed 16 Aug 2020), memorial 114919606, Isabelle Chatfield (1860-1943), Adams Cemetery, Troy, Walworth County, Wisconsin; gravestone walked by AGruling of the East Troy Area Historical Society.

[163] Ibid.

[164] "Milwaukee, Wisconsin Deaths, 1854-1911," database with images, *Ancestry* (https://www.ancestry.com : accessed 10 Aug 2020), Omer C Chatfield, 20 Jun 1908; "Word was Received," obituary, *The Whitewater Gazette* (Whitewater, Wisconsin), 23 Jul 1908, Omer Chatfield, p. 8, digital image, *Irvin L. Young Memorial Library Community History Archive* (http://irvinlyoung.advantage-preservation.com/ : accessed 31 Aug 2020).

[165] Alice Chatfield Gonia Family Bible, 1872.

[166] Seneca Chatfield Family Bible, 1873.

[167] "Makie C Martin," obituary, *The Arizona Republic*, Sun, 18 Jan 1959, p. 17, *Newspapers* (https://www.newspapers.com : accessed 16 Aug 2020).

1959 in Phoenix, Maricopa County, Arizona.[168] She was buried in Greenwood Memorial Cemetery.[169] DeWitt died 2 Jun 1921 in Milwaukee, Milwaukee County, Wisconsin,[170] and he was buried in Evergreen Cemetery, Troy.[171]

vi. JANE ELECTA CHATFIELD was born 22 Feb 1864 in Troy.[172] Jane died on 29 Jun 1871[173] after her clothes caught fire from sparks flying out of the stove.[174] Jane was napping in the stove room, when Silas came inside to start a fire in the stove for the evening.[175] Silas had gone back out to the barn, heard Jane screaming as she ran out of the house with her clothes on fire, and Silas and one of her brothers quickly extinguished the flames and removed her burnt clothes.[176] Medical aid was administered to Jane all night, but she died the next morning.[177] She was buried in Adams Cemetery.[178]

---

[168] Arizona Certificate of Death (1959), Makie Chatfield Martin, Arizona State Department of Health, Phoenix.

[169] "Makie C Martin," obituary, *The Arizona Republic*, Sun, 18 Jan 1959, p. 17, *Newspapers* (https://www.newspapers.com : accessed 16 Aug 2020).

[170] Wisconsin Original Certificate of Death (1921), De Witte Clinton Chatfield, Department of Health, Madison.

[171] *Find A Grave*. Database with images. (http://www.findagrave.com : accessed 10 Aug 2020), memorial 110779104, DeWitt C Chatfield (1862-1921), Evergreen Cemetery, Troy, Walworth County, Wisconsin; gravestone photograph by LKopet.

[172] Alice Chatfield Gonia Family Bible, 1872.

[173] Ibid.

[174] *History of Walworth County, Wisconsin*, 1882, p. 566.

[175] "Sad Accident," *Whitewater Register* (Whitewater, Wisconsin), 5 Jul 1871, p. 1, digital image, *Irvin L. Young Memorial Library Community History Archive* (http://irvinlyoung.advantage-preservation.com/ : accessed 1 Sep 2020).

[176] Ibid.

[177] Ibid.

[178] *Find A Grave*. Database with images. (http://www.findagrave.com : accessed 10 Aug 2020), memorial 114919690, Janie E Chatfield (1864-1871), Adams Cemetery, Troy, Walworth County, Wisconsin; gravestone photograph by PPatton.

vii.   SARAH ELIZABETH CHATFIELD was born 27 Jul 1869 in Troy.[179] Sarah was married to F Elmer Escher on 15 Apr 1900[180] in Colorado Springs, El Paso County, Colorado by the Reverend Edward Braislin.[181] Elmer was born in 1876, died on 25 May 1907 in Downers Grove, Du Page County, Illinois,[182] and he was buried in Oak Hill Cemetery in Downers Grove.[183] Sarah died on 29 Nov 1901,[184] and she was buried in Adams Cemetery.[185]

2.   viii.   ALICE JANE CHATFIELD was born 22 Jun 1873 in Troy.[186] Alice married Levi R Gonia on 16 Feb 1893 in Palmyra, Wisconsin.[187] Levi was born 19 Aug 1872 in Renfrew, Ontario, Canada, died 22 Oct 1947 in Whitewater, Walworth County, Wisconsin, and he was buried in Adams

---

[179] Alice Chatfield Gonia Family Bible, 1872; "Elizabeth Chatfield Escher," obituary, *The Whitewater Register* (Whitewater, Wisconsin), 12 Dec 1901, p. 8, digital image, *Irvin L. Young Memorial Library Community History Archive* (http://irvinlyoung.advantage-preservation.com/ : accessed 31 Aug 2020).
[180] Seneca Chatfield Family Bible, 1873.
[181] "Colorado Statewide Marriages, 1853-2006, Marriage Record" database with images, *FamilySearch* (https://www.familysearch.org : accessed 10 Aug 2020), F E Escher to S E Catfield, 15 Apr 1900, Colorado Springs, El Paso County, Colorado.
[182] "Death of Elmer Escher," obituary, *Downers Grove Reporter*, Illinois, Sat, 1 Jun 1907, p. 1. *Downers Grove Public Library* (http://vitacollections.ca/ : accessed 17 Aug 2020).
[183] *Find A Grave*. Database with images. (http://www.findagrave.com : accessed 17 Aug 2020), memorial 16270979, F. Elmer Escher (1876-1907), Oak Hill Cemetery, Downers Grove, Du Page County, Illinois; gravestone photograph by Icedobe.
[184] Alice Chatfield Gonia Family Bible, 1872.
[185] "Elizabeth Chatfield Escher," obituary, *The Whitewater Register* (Whitewater, Wisconsin), 12 Dec 1901, p. 8, digital image, *Irvin L. Young Memorial Library Community History Archive* (http://irvinlyoung.advantage-preservation.com/ : accessed 31 Aug 2020); *Find A Grave*. Database with images. (http://www.findagrave.com : accessed 10 Aug 2020), memorial 114919690, Libbie Chatfield Escher (1869-1901), Adams Cemetery, Troy, Walworth County, Wisconsin; gravestone photograph by PPatton.
[186] Alice Chatfield Gonia Family Bible, 1872.
[187] Marriage Certificate (1893). Levi R Gonia to Alice Chatfield, 16 Feb 1893, Palmyra, Wisconsin.

Cemetery.[188] Alice died 7 Jan 1937 in Whitewater.[189] Alice was buried in Adams Cemetery.[190]

viv.   SENECA BURCHARD CHATFIELD was born 15 Nov 1875 in Troy.[191] Seneca was married to Ella M Rhodes on 4 Dec 1907 in East Troy Township, Wisconsin, by the Reverend W J Agnew of Sherry, Wisconsin.[192] Ella was born 9 Nov 1882 in Mukwonago, Waukesha County, Wisconsin, died 15 Feb 1970 in Burlington, Racine County, Wisconsin, and she was buried in Adams Cemetery.[193] Seneca died 5 Jan 1961 in Geneva, Walworth County, Wisconsin.[194] Seneca was buried in Adams Cemetery.[195]

---

[188] Wisconsin Original Certificate of Death (1947), Levi R Gonia, Department of Health, Madison; Parents named on his death certificate were Robert Gonia and Katharine Murphy, all born in Renfrew, Canada. "Levi Gonia, 75, Died Here on Wednesday," obituary, *The Whitewater Register* (Whitewater, Wisconsin), 30 Oct 1947, p. 1, digital image, *Irvin L. Young Memorial Library Community History Archive* (http://irvinlyoung.advantage-preservation.com/ : accessed 31 Aug 2020).

[189] Wisconsin Original Certificate of Death (1937), Alice Jane Gonia, Department of Health, Madison.

[190] "Mrs. Gonia, 63, of Whitewater, Dies," obituary, *Janesville Daily Gazette*, Wisconsin, 7 Jan 1937, p2.

[191] Seneca Chatfield Family Bible, 1873.

[192] Ibid.

[193] "Mrs. Ella Chatfield," obituary, *Janesville Daily Gazette*, Wisconsin, Mon, 17 Feb 1970, p. 4, *Newspapers* (https://www.newspapers.com : accessed 16 Aug 2020).

[194] Wisconsin Original Certificate of Death (1961), Seneca B Chatfield, Department of Health, Madison.

[195] *Find A Grave*. Database with images. (http://www.findagrave.com : accessed 10 Aug 2020), memorial 50884488, Seneca B Chatfield (1875-1961), Adams Cemetery, Troy, Walworth County, Wisconsin; gravestone photograph by RPete.

SECOND GENERATION

2. **ALICE JANE CHATFIELD**, the daughter of Silas Barnum Chatfield and Catherine Gasper Kling was born 22 Jun 1873 in Troy.[196] She died 7 Jan 1937 in Whitewater, Wisconsin.[197] Alice married **LEVI R GONIA** on 16 Feb 1893 in Palmyra, Wisconsin.[198] Levi, the son of Robert Gonia and Catherine Murphy, was born 19 Aug 1872 in Renfrew, Ontario, Canada and appears to be the child named Olivier who was born on the same day and baptized Olivier Ganier on 15 Sep 1872 at St. James the Less Parish in Eganville, Renfrew County, Ontario, Canada to parents Robert Ganier and Catherine Murphy.[199] Levi died 22 Oct 1947 in Whitewater.[200] Alice and Levi are buried in Adams Cemetery.[201]

---

[196] Alice Chatfield Gonia Family Bible, 1872; Seneca Chatfield Family Bible, 1873; "Mrs. Gonia, 63, of Whitewater, Dies," obituary; "Aged Pioneer Passes Away," obituary, Silas B Chatfield; "Catheryn G Chatfield," obituary, *The East Troy News*, Wisconsin, 1 Aug 1915; 1880 U.S. Census, Walworth County, Wisconsin, population schedule, Troy, p. 225B, Enumeration District 236, Silas B Chatfield; database with images, Ancestry (www.ancestry.com : accessed 18 Aug 2020), citing NARA microfilm T9, roll 1450; *History of Walworth County, Wisconsin*, 1882, p. 566; Albert Clayton Beckwith, *History of Walworth County, Wisconsin*, vol 2, p. 998.

[197] Wisconsin Original Certificate of Death (1937), Alice Jane Gonia, Department of Health, Madison.

[198] Marriage Certificate (1893). Levi R Gonia to Alice Chatfield, 16 Feb 1893, Palmyra, Wisconsin.

[199] *FamilySearch* (https://www.familysearch.org/ark:/61903/3:1:33S7-9YWC-433?i=87&wc=M6VT-6Z9%3A220999401%2C221068601%2C221068602%2C221074701&cc=1927566 : accessed 11 Jun 2023), database with images, image 88 of 165, "Ontario, Roman Catholic Church Records, 1760-1923, Renfrew County" Register of St. James Parish, Eganville, 1866-1878, baptized Olivier Ganier on 15 Sep 1872, p. 138.

[200] Wisconsin Original Certificate of Death (1947), Levi R Gonia, Department of Health, Madison; Parents named on his death certificate were Robert Gonia and Katharine Murphy, all born in Renfrew, Canada. "Levi Gonia, 75, Died Here on Wednesday," obituary.

[201] "Mrs. Gonia, 63, of Whitewater, Dies," obituary; His burial- Wisconsin Original Certificate of Death (1947), Levi R Gonia, Department of Health, Madison.

Biographical Sketch of Alice Jane Chatfield and Levi R Gonia

Alice Jane Chatfield first appears in 1880 with her father Silas, who was working as a farmer, and her mother Catherine, who was keeping house. [202] Alice's older brothers, Levi and DeWitt were working on the farm, her older sister Sarah Elizabeth "Libbie" was attending school, and Alice and her younger brother Seneca were not old enough to attend school yet.[203] Alice married Levi R Gonia on 16 Feb 1893 in Palmyra, Jefferson County, Wisconsin,[204] and their first child,

The Gonia Family:
Kathryn, Levi, Gladys, and Alice
[Courtesy of Karl and Janet Olson]

Kathryn was born premature on 29 July 1893,[205] when their horse and wagon tipped over.[206]

Alice's mother Catherine "Grandma" Chatfield delivered all of her children, and according to Catherine's old medical record book, baby Kathryn only weighed two pounds when she was born.[207] The doctor told the family that it was unlikely the baby would live, but according to a 2006 newspaper article, Alice's mother, Catherine placed the tiny

[202] 1880 U.S. Census, Walworth County, Wisconsin, population schedule, Troy, p. 225B.

[203] Ibid.

[204] Marriage Certificate (1893). Levi R Gonia to Alice Chatfield, 16 Feb 1893, Palmyra, Wisconsin.

[205] "Midwife Helped Deliver Over 100 Babies Here!" *The East Troy News*, Wisconsin, 18 Mar 1970.

[206] "Remember When," *The Whitewater Register* (Whitewater, Wisconsin), 7 Jun 2012, p. 2, digital image, *Irvin L. Young Memorial Library Community History Archive* (http://irvinlyoung.advantage-preservation.com/ : accessed 31 Aug 2020).

[207] "Midwife Helped Deliver Over 100 Babies Here!" *The East Troy News*, Wisconsin, 18 Mar 1970.

baby in a shoebox, kept her inside the oven to keep her warm, and Kathryn survived.[208]

Alice and Levi's second child Arthur, was also born premature on 11 Jun 1896,[209] but he wasn't as lucky as Kathryn and died less than a year later.[210] The Gonia family moved into the Chatfield home on 6 Apr 1897,[211] and a few years later Alice, Levi and Kathryn were living with Levi's sister Mayme and next door to Alice's parents in 1900, where Levi worked as a day laborer.[212]

Alice gave birth to daughter, Maude Gladys Gonia in January 1903,[213] and a month later on 11 Feb, Silas and Catherine sold 81 hundredths

The Gonia Family- Back Row: Kathryn Gonia Olson,
Levi Gonia, Gerald Olson. Front Row seated: Robert
and Catherine Murphy Gonia
[Courtesy of Karl and Janet Olson]

[208] "Remember When," *The Whitewater Register* (Whitewater, Wisconsin), 7 Sep 2006, p. 5, digital image, *Irvin L. Young Memorial Library Community History Archive* (http://irvinlyoung.advantage-preservation.com/ : accessed 31 Aug 2020).

[209] "Midwife Helped Deliver Over 100 Babies Here!" *The East Troy News*, Wisconsin, 18 Mar 1970.

[210] *Find A Grave.* Database with images. (http://www.findagrave.com : accessed 21 Aug 2020), memorial 140534706, Arthur L Gonia (1896-1897), Adams Cemetery, Troy, Walworth County, Wisconsin.

[211] "It's Not Quite May 1st," *The Whitewater Register* (Whitewater, Wisconsin), 8 Apr 1897, p. 8, digital image, *Irvin L. Young Memorial Library Community History Archive* (http://irvinlyoung.advantage-preservation.com/ : accessed 31 Aug 2020).

[212] 1900 U.S. Census, Walworth County, Wisconsin, population schedule, Troy, p. 8B, Enumeration District 99, Levi R Gonia; database with images, Ancestry (www.ancestry.com : accessed 21 Aug 2020), citing NARA microfilm T623.

[213] Wisconsin Original Birth Certificate- Delayed (1903), Maude Gladys Gonia, Department of Health, Madison.

of an acre of the Chatfield farm to their daughter, Alice Jane Gonia for the sum of $1.00.[214] Both Alice and Levi could read and write, and that ability was passed on to both of the Gonia children.[215]

Levi, son of Robert Gonia and Catherine Murphy, was born 19 Aug 1872 in Renfrew County, Ontario, Canada.[216] Levi appears to be the child named Olivier Ganier, son of Robert Ganier and Catherine Murphy with the same birth date who was baptized on 15 Sep 1872 at St. James the Less Parish in Eganville, Renfrew County, Ontario, Canada.[217]

---

[214] *FamilySearch* (https://www.familysearch.org/ark:/61903/3:1:3Q9M-CSL2-CQNY?i=758&cat=571568 : accessed 2 Sep 2020), digital film 8549052, images 439 of 801, "Deeds, 1839-1921; Indexes 1839-1901," Troy, Walworth County, Wisconsin, Register of Deeds, vol. 108, p. 268, Silas B Chatfield and Catherine Chatfield, his wife of Troy to Alice Jane Gonia of Troy, signed 11 Feb 1903, recorded 19 Feb 1903.

[215] 1910 U.S. Census, Rock County, Wisconsin, population schedule, Johnstown, p. 4A, Enumeration District 120, Levi Gonia; database with images, *Ancestry* (www.ancestry.com : accessed 24 Aug 2020); and 1920 U.S. Census, Koochiching County, Minnesota, population schedule, International Falls, p. 2A, Enumeration District 52, John Nagle; database with images, *Ancestry* (www.ancestry.com : accessed 10 Sep 2020).

[216] Wisconsin Original Certificate of Death (1947), Levi R Gonia, Department of Health, Madison; and 1920 U.S. Census, Koochiching County, Minnesota, population schedule, International Falls, p. 2A, Enumeration District 52, Levi Gonia, database with images, *Ancestry* (www.ancestry.com : accessed 24 Aug 2020); 1881 Canada Census, Admaston, Renfrew South, Ontario, Canada, District Number 13, p. 14, Robert Geunew; database with images, *Ancestry* (www.ancestry.com : accessed 24 Aug 2020).

[217] *FamilySearch* (https://www.familysearch.org/ark:/61903/3:1:33S7-9YWC-433?i=87&wc=M6VT-6Z9%3A220999401%2C221068601%2C221068602%2C221074701&cc=1927566 : accessed 11 Jun 2023), database with images, image 88 of 165, "Ontario, Roman Catholic Church Records, 1760-1923, Renfrew County," Register of St. James Parish, Eganville, 1866-1878, baptized Olivier Ganier on 15 Sep 1872, p. 138.

Robert's surname was found spelled various ways: Gonia, Gania, Guinie, Geunew and Gagnon.[218] Robert was born in Admaston, Renfrew County, Ontario, Canada on 17 Mar 1846,[219] and he is likely the same Robert who was baptized in Kemptville, Ontario, Canada at seven months old on 22 October 1846 to parents Levie Ganné and Ellen Keys of Montague, Ontario, Canada.[220]

Levi's mother Catherine appears to be the Catherine Murphy who was born in Griffith, Renfrew County, Ontario, Canada on 22 Mar 1851 to Irish immigrant parents, Christopher Croghan Murphy and Julia

---

[218] *FamilySearch* (https://www.familysearch.org/ark:/61903/3:1:3Q9M-CS76-79YB-Z?i=24&wc=Q866-ZCG%3A1589662454%2C1589662470&cc=2568642 : accessed 12 Jun 2023), database with images, image 25 of 46, vol. 60, "Ontario County Marriage Registers, 1858-1869, Renfrew County," p. 23, Robert Gagnon to Catherine Murphy, 16 Sep 1867. Robert Gagnon, son of Levi Gagnon and Ellen Keece; Robert began using the Gonia spelling by 1910.

[219] Wisconsin Original Certificate of Death (1938), Robert Gonia, Department of Health, Madison.

[220] "Ontario, Canada, Roman Catholic Baptisms, Marriages, and Burials, 1760-1923," *Ancestry* (https://www.ancestry.com/discoveryui-content/view/809226:61505?ssrc=pt&tid=165564285&pid=372149369853 : accessed 18 Jun 2023), database with images, image 31 of 456, Kemptville > Not Stated >Burial, Baptism, Marriage, Confirmation, Visitation; Kemptville, p. 31; 1844-1910; Robert's baptism, marriage and death records show his parents to be Levie Ganné [looks like Louis] and Ellen Keys, Levi Gagnon and Ellen Keece, and Levi Gonia and Ellen Conlon, respectively. Conlon appears to be an error on the death certificate, as the marriage record of Levi Gagnon shows Ellen's maiden name as Quesse/Keys. Levi and Ellen's three youngest children were all baptized in Kemptville; see also "Québec, Canada, Vital and Church Records, Drouin Collection, 1621-1968," *Ancestry* (https://www.ancestry.com/imageviewer/collections/1091/images/d13p_012407 72?pId=4634425 : accessed 12 Jun 2023), database with images, image 18 of 37, Saint > St-Jacques-l'Achigan > ALL > 1827, Marriage of Olivier Gagnon to Heleine Quesse [Helen Keys], 19 Jun 1827.

Moriarty and was baptized on 26 May 1851 at Mount St Patrick, Ontario, Canada.[221]

Renfrew County adjoins the west bank of the Ottawa River in southern Ontario,[222] and Admaston sits near Ontario's border with Québec.[223] Robert Gonia's father is likely French Canadian, Olivier (Levi) Gagnon, son of Jean Baptiste Gagnon and Marie Anne Légaré, who was baptized on 22 Mar 1807 in St-Jacques-l'Achigan, Québec,[224] and Olivier (Levi) was married to Heleine Quesse (sometimes shown as Helen Keys) on 19 June 1827 in St-Jacques-l'Achigan, Québec.[225] Olivier Gagnon's lineage can be traced back to Québec immigrant Mathurin Gagnon, as well as other early settlers of Québec, including Abraham Martin who arrived in 1620 and Pierre Desportes, who arrived in 1619.[226]

---

[221] Wisconsin Original Certificate of Death (1940), Catherine Murphy Gonia, Department of Health, Madison; and "Ontario, Canada, Roman Catholic Baptisms, Marriages, and Burials, 1760-1923" *Ancestry* (https://www.ancestry.com/imageviewer/collections/61505/images/FS_0051068 52_00095?pId=979235 : accessed 12 Jun 2012), database with images, image 91 of 685, baptism, Mount St Patrick > Saint Patrick > Various Church Records, Mount St Patrick, 1846-51, 1866-1908, Catherine Murphy, 26 May 1851; her death certificate shows a birth date of 17 Mar 1851.

[222] *Wikipedia* (http://en.wikipedia.org : accessed 30 Aug 2020), "Renfrew County."

[223] *Wikipedia* (http://en.wikipedia.org : accessed 30 Aug 2020), "Admaston/Bromley."

[224] "Québec, Canada, Vital and Church Records, Drouin Collection, 1621-1968," *Ancestry* (https://www.ancestry.com/imageviewer/collections/1091/images/d13p_012400 69?pId=6377227 : accessed 12 Jun 2023), database with images, image 7 of 23, Saint > St-Jacques-l'Achigan > ALL > 1807, Olivier Gagnon, baptism, 22 Mar 1807.

[225] "Québec, Canada, Vital and Church Records, Drouin Collection, 1621-1968," *Ancestry* (https://www.ancestry.com/imageviewer/collections/1091/images/d13p_012407 72?pId=4634425 : accessed 12 Jun 2023), database with images, image 18 of 37, Saint > St-Jacques-l'Achigan > ALL > 1827, Marriage of Olivier Gagnon to Helene Quesse [Helen Keys], 19 Jun 1827.

[226] Denise R. Larson, *Companions of Champlain, Founding Families of Quebec, 1608-1635* (Baltimore, Maryland: Clearfield Company, 2018); also, personal research of the author; lineage traced through vital records to early Québec settlers.

In the last part of the 19th century, French Canadians began migrating to Eastern Ontario due to overpopulation and unemployment in Québec.[227] By the 1840's most of Québec's fertile farmland had been taken, and thousands of landless farmers searched for new locations that offered affordable and fertile land.[228]

Robert and Catherine Gonia in Canada
[Courtesy of Karl and Janet Olson]

By 1930, nearly one million French Canadians from the Provinces of Québec and Ontario left Canada and emigrated to the United States.[229] Unlike many French Canadians who emigrated to New England to obtain temporary work in factories, many French Canadians who headed for and settled in the U.S. Midwest never returned to Canada.[230]

---

[227] *Québec History* (http://faculty.marianopolis.edu/c.belanger/quebechistory/readings/leaving.htm : accessed 30 Aug 2020), "French Canadian Emigration to the United States 1840-1930."

[228] Ibid.

[229] *Vermont History* (https://vermonthistory.org/ : accessed 30 Aug 2020), "French Canadian Immigration to Vermont and New England (1840-1930)."

[230] *French American Heritage Foundation of Minnesota (*http://fahfminn.org/ : accessed 30 Aug 2020), "The Influence of the French Canadians on the US Midwest," p. 2.

Although Levi was baptized Catholic,[231] and his grandfather was born and raised Catholic in Québec and later Ontario,[232] Levi did not appear to have been a practicing Catholic after 1881.[233]

Levi's obituary did not mention his religion at the time of his death.[234] His wife Alice was not raised Catholic,[235] which may have been a contributing factor, and Alice's funeral services were held at Adams Church.[236] Levi and Alice's daughter Kathryn would later marry in the Lutheran Church,[237] and Kathryn would remain active in the Lutheran faith as an adult.[238]

Levi remained in Admaston with his parents until they, like other French Canadians emigrated to the United States. Robert emigrated ahead of the family to Albion, Jackson County, Wisconsin in 1881, and Catherine and their five children emigrated the following year.[239] At the age of seventeen, Levi found himself in trouble with the law while living in Jackson County, and in 1889 he was sentenced to reform

---

[231] 1881 Canada Census, Admaston, Renfrew South, Ontario, Canada, District Number 13, p. 14, Robert Geunew; database with images, *Ancestry* (www.ancestry.com : accessed 24 Aug 2020).

[232] "Québec, Canada, Vital and Church Records (Drouin Collection), 1621-1968," Olivier Gagnon, 22 Mar 1807, *Ancestry* (https://www.ancestry.com/ : accessed 29 Jul 2020).

[233] 1881 Canada Census, Admaston, Renfrew South, Ontario, Canada, District Number 13, p. 14, Robert Geunew; database with images, *Ancestry* (www.ancestry.com : accessed 24 Aug 2020).

[234] "Levi Gonia, 75, Died Here on Wednesday," obituary.

[235] Al Gruling, "Town of Troy History," *Town of Troy*.

[236] "Mrs. Gonia, 63, of Whitewater, Dies," obituary.

[237] "U. S. Evangelical Lutheran Church of America, Records, 1875-1940," *Ancestry* (https://www.ancestry.com/imageviewer/collections/60722/images/41742_31494 3-00249?pId=10896015 : accessed 12 Jun 2023), database with images, image 77 of 120, Congregational Records > Wisconsin > Whitewater > Heart Prairie Lutheran Church, Marriages, Kathryn M Gonia to Hjalmer N Olson, 10 Jan 1911.

[238] "First Lutheran Holds its Annual Business Meeting," *The Whitewater Register* (Whitewater, Wisconsin), 11 Jan 1945, p. 1, digital image, *Irvin L. Young Memorial Library Community History Archive* (http://irvinlyoung.advantage-preservation.com/ : accessed 31 Aug 2020); "Ladies Aid Society," *The Whitewater Register*, Wisconsin, 27 Sep 1951, p. 4 (http://irvinlyoung.advantage-preservation.com/ : accessed 31 Aug 2020).

[239] "Married 72 Years" *The La Crosse Tribune*, Wisconsin, Mon, 19 Sep 1938.

school for attempted assault.[240] Once he was released from reform school, he appears to have stayed out of trouble, at least serious trouble, for the remainder of his life.

On 25 Feb 1899, Levi's father Robert purchased 60 acres of railroad land in Albion from the Chicago, St. Paul, Minneapolis & Omaha Railway Company.[241] Levi's seven youngest siblings were born in Wisconsin,[242] and Robert and Catherine Gonia remained in Albion until their deaths on 11 Dec 1938 and 19 May 1940, respectively[243].

Levi Gonia's 1913 U. S. Naturalization petition indicated that he arrived at the port of Detroit crossing over from Windsor, Ontario, Canada via the Grand Trunk Railway.[244] The Grand Trunk Railway was a train system that operated in the Canadian provinces of Québec and

---

240 "The Northwest Condensed," *Argus-Leader* (Sioux Falls, South Dakota), 28 Sep 1889, p. 1, col. 2: digital image, *Newspapers* (https://www.newspapers.com : accessed 13 Jun 2023).

241 Jackson County, Wisconsin, Deed Record, Deed Book 56, p. 197, #43413, Chicago, St. Paul, Minneapolis & Omaha Railway Company to Robert Gonia, signed 25 Feb 1899, recorded 23 Mar 1899, Jackson County Register of Deeds; "Married 72 Years" *The La Crosse Tribune*, Wisconsin, Mon, 19 Sep 1938, *Newspapers* (https://www.newspapers.com : accessed 26 Aug 2020).

242 "Married 72 Years" *The La Crosse Tribune*, Wisconsin, Mon, 19 Sep 1938.

243 Wisconsin Original Certificate of Death (1938), Robert Gonia, Department of Health, Madison; Wisconsin Original Certificate of Death (1940), Catherine Gonia, Department of Health, Madison; "Married 72 Years" *The La Crosse Tribune*, Wisconsin, Mon, 19 Sep 1938; Jackson County, Wisconsin Register in Probate, Estate Record of Robert Gonia, No. 163456, vol. 63, p. 9, vol. 138, p. 509, and Estate Record of Catherine Gonia, No. 163457, vol. 63, p. 8, vol. 138, p. 510, both recorded on 25 Jul 1950, Jackson County Courthouse.

244 *FamilySearch* (https://www.familysearch.org/ark:/61903/3:1:3QS7-893Z-6P84?i=93&cc=2046887 : accessed 12 Aug 2023), database with images, images 94 and 95 of 560, "Wisconsin, County Naturalization Records, 1807-1992, Walworth," Levi Gonia, 1 Jun 1914. Levi attested on this record that he emigrated on or about Nov 1880, but that year is incorrect, as he was still living in Canada in the 1881 census with his parents. His sister Mayme who is living with him in 1900 was born in May 1882 in Canada, and the 1900 census, as well as numerous other census and records, including his parents' 72-year anniversary newspaper article, give the immigration year as 1882. Levi's petition was denied 30 June 1914, when the court found he had falsely represented himself as a U. S. Citizen on his intoxicating liquors license in 1913.

Ontario, some New England states, and Michigan.[245] The towns of Admaston and Windsor are roughly 400 miles apart, but the Gonia family could have conceivably traveled by train most of the way, as the Grand Trunk Railway was fairly extensive at the time.[246] Because of the development of the railway within Québec, Ontario and the upper portion of the United States, emigration became relatively inexpensive and fast for many French Canadians to emigrate to the United States.[247]

Unlike his father-in-law Silas Chatfield, who lived in the same town for almost sixty-two years, Levi Gonia moved frequently with his family, likely in search of better employment. Levi's varied career included occupations ranging from saloon keeper[248] to tractor engine operator[249] to paper mill engineer.[250] In Sept 1904, Levi began working as an engineer at the sorghum mill on his father-in-law Silas' farm.[251] In 1905, Levi and Alice moved with their two daughters and became residents

---

[245] *Wikipedia* (http://en.wikipedia.org : accessed 26 Aug 2020), "Grand Trunk Railway."

[246] *Wikipedia* (http://en.wikipedia.org : accessed 26 Aug 2020), "GTR, 1885 map."

[247] *Québec History* (http://faculty.marianopolis.edu/c.belanger/quebechistory/pictures/birdseye.htm : accessed 30 Aug 2020), "Bird's Eye View, Union Station, Manchester NH (circa 1915).".

[248] *FamilySearch* (https://www.familysearch.org/ark:/61903/3:1:3QS7-893Z-6P84?i=93&cc=2046887 : accessed 12 Aug 2023), database with images, images 94 and 95 of 560, "Wisconsin, County Naturalization Records, 1807-1992, Walworth," Levi Gonia, 1 Jun 1914.

[249] "Levi Gonia Left Saturday," *The Whitewater Register* (Whitewater, Wisconsin), 17 Jul 1919, p. 4, digital image, *Irvin L. Young Memorial Library Community History Archive* (http://irvinlyoung.advantage-preservation.com/ : accessed 3 Sep 2020).

[250] 1920 U.S. Census, Koochiching County, Minnesota, population schedule, International Falls, p. 2A, Enumeration District 52, Levi Gonia; database with images, Ancestry (www.ancestry.com : accessed 24 Aug 2020), citing NARA microfilm T625, roll 842.

[251] "Levi Gonia Commenced," *The Whitewater Register* (Whitewater, Wisconsin), 30 Sep 1904, p. 5, digital image, *Irvin L. Young Memorial Library Community History Archive* (http://irvinlyoung.advantage-preservation.com/ : accessed 31 Aug 2020).

of La Grange, Walworth County, Wisconsin where Levi started work as a farm laborer.[252]

Levi Gonia [Courtesy of Karl and Janet Olson]

By 1907, Levi had moved with his family to Johnstown, Rock County, Wisconsin where he was working as a farmer.[253] On 7 Nov 1907, a sixteen-year-old farm hand named Earl Baxter, of Fort Atkinson, who worked for Levi Gonia on his farm in Johnstown, attempted to assault Kathryn's younger sister Maude.[254]

Levi immediately contacted the Janesville sheriff, and after a couple of days of searching for Earl, he was finally found and arrested on 9 Nov 1907.[255] His bail was set at $800.00, but Earl's mother was unable to furnish the bond.[256] A physician testified that Maude was not physically injured during the attempted

[252] 1905 Wisconsin State Census, Walworth County, La Grange, p. 251, Levi P Gonia; database with images, Ancestry (www.ancestry.com : accessed 24 Aug 2020).

[253] 1910 U.S. Census, Rock County, Wisconsin, population schedule, Johnstown, p. 4A, Enumeration District 120, Levi Gonia; database with images, Ancestry (www.ancestry.com : accessed 24 Aug 2020), citing NARA microfilm T624, roll 1735.

[254] "Baxter Sent to Green Bay," *The Whitewater Register* (Whitewater, Wisconsin), 15 Nov 1907, p. 3, digital image, *Irvin L. Young Memorial Library Community History Archive* (http://irvinlyoung.advantage-preservation.com/ : accessed 21 Sep 2020).

[255] "Baxter Sent to Green Bay," *The Whitewater Register.*

[256] "A Serious Charge," *The Whitewater Gazette* (Whitewater, Wisconsin), 14 Nov 1907, p. 1, digital image, *Irvin L. Young Memorial Library Community History Archive* (http://irvinlyoung.advantage-preservation.com/ : accessed 21 Sep 2020).

assault.[257] Earl denied the charge at the time of his arrest, but he subsequently pled guilty and was sentenced to two years at the Wisconsin State Reformatory in Green Bay.[258] The Wisconsin State Reformatory opened in 1898 and became the Green Bay Correctional Institution on 1 July 1979. [259]

On February 1913, Levi and Alice finally left Rock County and moved to Whitewater, Walworth, Wisconsin on 1 March 1913.[260] On 12 July 1913, Levi was working as a saloon keeper.[261] A fellow saloon keeper, W. A. Ludtke served as a witness on Levi's U. S. Naturalization paperwork and attested that Levi met the criteria necessary to become a citizen of the United States.[262] W. A. Ludtke was likely the Wm. August Luedtke of 51 South River, who on 30 June 1913 was one of forty-nine saloon owners whose saloon license was granted/renewed by the Janesville City Council in Walworth County.[263] On that same day in Whitewater, both Wm A Ludtke and Levi Gonia were granted

---

[257] "A Serious Charge," *The Whitewater Gazette* (Whitewater, Wisconsin), 14 Nov 1907, p. 1, digital image, *Irvin L. Young Memorial Library Community History Archive* (http://irvinlyoung.advantage-preservation.com/ : accessed 21 Sep 2020).

[258] "Baxter Sent to Green Bay," *The Whitewater Register* (Whitewater, Wisconsin), 15 Nov 1907, p. 3.

[259] *Wikipedia* (http://en.wikipedia.org : accessed 21 Sep 2020), "Green Bay Correctional Institution."

[260] "Levi Gonia will move to Whitewater," *The Whitewater Register* (Whitewater, Wisconsin), 14 Feb 1913, p. 5 (http://irvinlyoung.advantage-preservation.com/ : accessed 31 Aug 2020).

[261] *FamilySearch* (https://www.familysearch.org/ark:/61903/3:1:3QS7-893Z-6P84?i=93&cc=2046887 : accessed 12 Aug 2023), database with images, images 94 and 95 of 560, "Wisconsin, County Naturalization Records, 1807-1992, Walworth," Levi Gonia, 1 Jun 1914.

[262] *FamilySearch* (https://www.familysearch.org/ark:/61903/3:1:3QS7-893Z-6P84?i=93&cc=2046887 : accessed 12 Aug 2023), database with images, images 94 and 95 of 560, "Wisconsin, County Naturalization Records, 1807-1992, Walworth," Levi Gonia, 1 Jun 1914.

[263] "Forty-one Licenses for Saloons granted today at the Council Session," *Janesville Daily Gazette*, Wisconsin, 30 Jun 1913, p. 1, col. 1.

liquor licenses at the Whitewater Common Council meeting, where the license fee cost $500.00.[264]

In Levi's approved liquor license application addressed to the Mayor and the Common Council he asked that the license be granted:

> …to keep a saloon for the sale of strong, spirituous, malt, ardent and intoxicating liquors, in quantities of less than (1) gallon, to be drank on the premises. That the location of the premises where such business is to be conducted is No. 99 Center Street, City of Whitewater, Walworth County, Wisconsin.[265]

Unfortunately, Levi Gonia's U. S. Naturalization petition was denied on 30 June 1914, when the court determined that Levi falsely represented himself as a U. S. citizen when he applied for his intoxicating liquors license a year earlier. Levi was still falsely representing himself as a U. S. citizen on 16 September 1935, when he unsuccessfully attempted to help an acquaintance, a Mr. Sutherland with his own naturalization petition. During the hearing, the Deputy Clerk reviewed Levi's prior record from 1914, determined Levi was still not a U. S. Citizen, could not serve as a witness and denied Mr. Sutherland's request.[266]

The saloon industry would soon face an upheaval as the prohibition movement began to attract more and more supporters to the cause.[267] By 1917, the U. S. Congress finished work on its prohibition

---

[264] "Council Proceeding," *The Whitewater Register* (Whitewater, Wisconsin), 30 Jun 1913, p. 3, digital image, *Irvin L. Young Memorial Library Community History Archive* (http://irvinlyoung.advantage-preservation.com/ : accessed 31 Aug 2020).

[265] "Levi Gonia," *The Whitewater Register* (Whitewater, Wisconsin), 20 Jun 1913, p. 8, digital image, *Irvin L. Young Memorial Library Community History Archive* (http://irvinlyoung.advantage-preservation.com/ : accessed 31 Aug 2020).

[266] "Wisconsin, County Naturalization Records, 1807-1992, Walworth" database with images, *FamilySearch* (https://www.familysearch.org : accessed 24 Aug 2020), Levi Gonia, 1 Jun 1914.

[267] *Wikipedia* (http://en.wikipedia.org : accessed 26 Aug 2020), "Prohibition in the United States."

amendment, and prohibition became federal law on 29 Jan 1919 with the ratification of the 18th Amendment.[268] The enforcement of prohibition was not particularly effective, and residents during this time could find liquor in soft drink parlors, and doctors were allowed to "prescribe" medicinal alcohol for patients.[269] Prohibition would officially end on 5 Dec 1933 with the ratification of the 21st Amendment.[270]

Alice Chatfield Gonia
[Courtesy of Karl and Janet Olson]

Levi left the saloon business, and he took work where he could get it. In May 1918, Levi was working in Aberdeen, South Dakota as a tractor engine operator and was apparently living there by himself, because later that month Alice traveled to South Dakota to stay with him for the summer.[271] Levi was still performing some tractor engine work in Aberdeen in 1919, so he was making trips back and forth between Aberdeen from Walworth County to do so.[272] By 1920

[268] *Wisconsin History* (http://www.wisconsinhistory.org : accessed 26 Aug 2020), "Prohibition."

[269] *Wikipedia* (http://en.wikipedia.org : accessed 26 Aug 2020), "Prohibition in the United States."

[270] Ibid.

[271] "Mrs. Gonia in Aberdeen, South Dakota," *The Whitewater Register* (Whitewater, Wisconsin), 24 May 1918, p. 4; digital image, *Irvin L. Young Memorial Library Community History Archive* (http://irvinlyoung.advantage-preservation.com/ : accessed 31 Aug 2020).

[272] "Levi Gonia Left Saturday," *The Whitewater Register* (Whitewater, Wisconsin), 17 Jul 1919, p. 4, digital image, *Irvin L. Young Memorial Library Community History Archive* (http://irvinlyoung.advantage-preservation.com/ : accessed 3 Sep 2020). Levi does not appear in any Aberdeen directories during this time.

Levi had settled in International Falls, Koochiching, Minnesota with Alice, as his two daughters were married by then, and he began working as an engineer in the paper mill.[273] The village of Koochiching was incorporated on 10 Aug 1901, and the name was changed to International Falls on 1 Jan 1903. [274]

Wealthy business entrepreneur Edward W Backus completed the construction of the hydroelectric dam at Koochiching Falls, along with his four-machine newsprint mill in 1910.[275] By 1914, the mill began producing insulate, and employment opportunities in the area were plentiful and likely attractive to future workers.[276] By the mid-1920s, Backus' plans for expansion would be hindered by conservationists, court battles and the stock market crash of 1929, ultimately putting an end to the Backus empire. [277]

---

[273] 1920 U.S. Census, Koochiching County, Minnesota, population schedule, International Falls, p. 2A, Enumeration District 52, Levi Gonia; database with images, Ancestry (www.ancestry.com : accessed 24 Aug 2020), citing NARA microfilm T625, roll 842.

[274] *Wikipedia* (http://en.wikipedia.org : accessed 30 Aug 2020), "International Falls, Minnesota."

[275] *Koochiching County, Minnesota* (https://www.co.koochiching.mn.us/222/The-Era-of-EW-Backus : accessed 30 Aug 2020), "The Era of E.W. Backus."

[276] *City of International Falls, Minnesota* (https://www.ci.international-falls.mn.us/about-international-falls/ : accessed 30 Aug 2020), "History of International Falls."

[277] *Koochiching County, Minnesota*, "The Era of E.W. Backus."

Table 3
Levi R Gonia: Occupations and Residences

Year and Source	Occupation	Residence
1881 Census of Canada[a]	None given	Admaston, Ontario, Canada
1895 Wisconsin State Census[b]	None given	Troy, Walworth, WI
1900 U. S. Census[c]	Day laborer	Troy, Walworth, WI
1904 *The Whitewater Register*[d]	Sorghum Mill Engineer	Troy, Walworth, WI
1905 Wisconsin State Census[e]	Farm Laborer	La Grange, Walworth, WI
1910 U. S. Census[f]	Farmer	Johnstown, Rock County, WI
1913 *The Whitewater Register*[g]	Farm Laborer	Utter's Corner, Rock, WI
1913 U. S. Petition of Naturalization[h]	Saloon Keeper	Whitewater, Walworth, WI
1918-9 *The Whitewater Register*[i]	Tractor Engine Operator	Aberdeen, Brown, SD
1920 U. S. Census[j]	Paper Mill Engineer	International Falls, MN
1930 U. S. Census[k] [Unemployed]	Construction Laborer	Whitewater, Walworth, WI
1940 U. S. Census[l] on 11 Apr 1940	None given	Whitewater, Walworth, WI
1940 U. S. Census[m] on 4 May 1940	None given	Shelby, Tippecanoe, IN

a. 1881 Canada Census, Admaston, Renfrew South, Ontario, Canada, District Number 13, p. 14, Robert Geunew; database with images, *Ancestry* (www.ancestry.com : accessed 24 Aug 2020).

b. 1895 Wisconsin State Census, Walworth County, Troy, p. 4, Levi R Gonia; database with images, *Ancestry* (www.ancestry.com : accessed 24 Aug 2020).

c. 1900 U.S. Census, Walworth County, Wisconsin, population schedule, Troy, p. 8B, Enumeration District 99, Levi R Gonia; database with images, *Ancestry* (www.ancestry.com : accessed 21 Aug 2020), citing NARA microfilm T623, roll 1821.

d. "Levi Gonia Commenced," *The Whitewater Register*, (Whitewater, Wisconsin), 30 Sep 1904, p. 5, digital image, (http://irvinlyoung.advantage-preservation.com/ : accessed 31 Aug 2020), Digital Archives at the Irvin L Young Memorial Library.

e. 1905 Wisconsin State Census, Walworth County, La Grange, p. 251, Levi P Gonia; database with images, *Ancestry* (www.ancestry.com : accessed 24 Aug 2020).

f. 1910 U.S. Census, Rock County, Wisconsin, population schedule, Johnstown, p. 4A, Enumeration District 120, Levi Gonia; database with images, *Ancestry* (www.ancestry.com : accessed 24 Aug 2020), citing NARA microfilm T624, roll 1735.

g. "Levi Gonia will move to Whitewater," *The Whitewater Register* (Whitewater, Wisconsin), 14 Feb 1913, p. 5, digital image, *Irvin L. Young Memorial Library Community History Archive* (http://irvinlyoung.advantage-preservation.com/ : accessed 31 Aug 2020).

h. "Wisconsin, County Naturalization Records, 1807-1992, Walworth" database with images, *FamilySearch* (https://www.familysearch.org : accessed 24 Aug 2020), Levi Gonia, signed on 12 Jul 1913.

i. "Mrs. Gonia in Aberdeen, South Dakota," *The Whitewater Register* (Whitewater, Wisconsin), 24 May 1918, p. 4 (http://irvinlyoung.advantage-preservation.com/ : accessed 31 Aug 2020); and "Levi Gonia Left Saturday," *The Whitewater Register* (Whitewater, Wisconsin), 17 Jul 1919, p. 4, digital image, *Irvin L. Young Memorial Library Community History Archive* (http://irvinlyoung.advantage-preservation.com/ : accessed 3 Sep 2020).

j. 1920 U.S. Census, Koochiching County, Minnesota, population schedule, International Falls, p. 2A, Enumeration District 52, Levi Gonia; database with images, *Ancestry* (www.ancestry.com : accessed 24 Aug 2020), citing NARA microfilm T625, roll 842.

k. 1930 U.S. Census, Walworth County, Wisconsin, population schedule, Whitewater, p. 4A, Enumeration District 31, Levi R Gonia; database with images, *Ancestry* (www.ancestry.com : accessed 24 Aug 2020), citing NARA microfilm T626. Col. 28 shows he is unemployed.

l. 1940 U.S. Census, Walworth County, Wisconsin, population schedule, Whitewater, p. 7A, Enumeration District 32, Levi Gonia; database with images, *Ancestry* (www.ancestry.com : accessed 24 Aug 2020), citing NARA microfilm T627, roll 4643.

m. 1940 U.S. Census, Tippecanoe County, Indiana, population schedule, Shelby, p. 61A, Enumeration District 30, Levi Gonia; database with images, *Ancestry* (www.ancestry.com : accessed 24 Aug 2020), citing NARA microfilm T627, roll 4643. He was enumerated a second time on 4 May 1940 living near his daughter Maude.

Levi Gonia purchased a home located on 115 North Prairie Street in Whitewater from the Jolley family in December 1928.[278] In April 1930, although Levi's occupational field was listed in the construction

The Gonia Family: Kathryn, Levi, and Gladys
[Courtesy of Karl and Janet Olson]

industry as a laborer, he was not employed at the time.[279] Levi's wife Alice died seven years later in Whitewater on 7 Jan 1937, [280] and Levi was still living at the same residence in October 1938.[281] Ten years later, Levi could be found living with his daughter Kathryn's family at the same Whitewater address on 11 April 1940.[282]

A few weeks later on the 4th of May, he was enumerated a second time living near his daughter Gladys Ralston [Maude] in Shelby,

[278] "The Jolley Home," *The Whitewater Register* (Whitewater, Wisconsin), 3 Jan 1929, p. 3, digital image, *Irvin L. Young Memorial Library Community History Archive* (http://irvinlyoung.advantage-preservation.com/ : accessed 3 Sep 2020).

[279] 1930 U.S. Census, Walworth County, Wisconsin, population schedule, Whitewater, p. 4A, Enumeration District 31, Levi R Gonia; database with images, Ancestry (www.ancestry.com : accessed 24 Aug 2020), citing NARA microfilm T626, roll 2667.

[280] Wisconsin Original Certificate of Death (1937), Alice Jane Gonia, Department of Health, Madison.

[281] Wisconsin Telephone Company. *Whitewater Telephone Directory, including Lima Center.* (Madison, Wisconsin : October 1938), p. 15.

[282] 1940 U.S. Census, Walworth County, Wisconsin, population schedule, Whitewater, p. 7A, Enumeration District 32, Levi Gonia; database with images, Ancestry (www.ancestry.com : accessed 24 Aug 2020), citing NARA microfilm T627, roll 4643.

Tippecanoe, Indiana.[283] Levi had moved back to 115 North Prairie Street in Whitewater by 1947.[284] He died in Whitewater on 22 Oct 1947.[285] Kathryn Olson was appointed executrix of her father's estate, which was finalized on 15 Jul 1948.[286] Levi's daughter Maude Gladys Ralston received a legacy of $1,000, and Levi's home remained in the possession of his daughter Kathryn.[287]

Alice Jane Chatfield and her husband, Levi Gonia enjoyed an active social life. A few newspaper excerpts include:

- Miss Bertha Rhodes is spending a few days with Mrs. Levi R Gonia[288]
- …The annual shoot ended Saturday, …Levi Gonia killd [sic] 48 crows… Gonia made the greatest score, 2,485…[289]
- Mrs. Alice Gonia and Miss Lillian Kennedy spent part of Thursday with Miss Ethyl Chatfield at Lake Beulah[290]

---

[283] 1940 U.S. Census, Tippecanoe County, Indiana, population schedule, Shelby, p. 61A, Enumeration District 30, Levi Gonia; database with images, Ancestry (www.ancestry.com : accessed 24 Aug 2020), citing NARA microfilm T627, roll 4643.

[284] Wisconsin Original Certificate of Death (1947), Levi R Gonia, Department of Health, Madison.

[285] Ibid.

[286] Walworth County, Wisconsin Register in Probate, Will and Probate Record for Levi Gonia, No. 21385, vol. 30, p. 48, vol. 225, p. 54, Final Judgment, 17 Jul 1948; the actual will was not in the probate file at Walworth County, Wisconsin, Courthouse, Elkhorn.

[287] Walworth County, Wisconsin Register in Probate, Will and Probate Record for Levi Gonia.

[288] "Miss Bertha Rhodes," *The Whitewater Register* (Whitewater, Wisconsin), 30 Jul 1896, p. 8, digital image, *Irvin L. Young Memorial Library Community History Archive* (http://irvinlyoung.advantage-preservation.com/ : accessed 31 Aug 2020).

[289] "The Annual Shoot," *The Whitewater Register* (Whitewater, Wisconsin), 2 Jun 1898, p. 8, digital image, *Irvin L. Young Memorial Library Community History Archive* (http://irvinlyoung.advantage-preservation.com/ : accessed 31 Aug 2020).

[290] "Mrs. Alice Gonia," *The Whitewater Register* (Whitewater, Wisconsin), 8 Feb 1900, p. 8, digital image, *Irvin L. Young Memorial Library Community History Archive* (http://irvinlyoung.advantage-preservation.com/ : accessed 31 Aug 2020).

- Mrs. Levi Gonia and daughter Kittie spent Wednesday and Thursday with Mrs. Katherine Tobin of Heart Prairie[291]
- Levi Gonia joined with the Groff boys last Saturday in fox hunting…[292]
- Mr. and Mrs. Fred Wunderlich of Utter's Corner entertained Mr. and Mrs. Merle Rice and family and Mr. and Mrs. Levi Gonia in honor of Mrs. Wunderlich's father, Frank Rice, of Wisconsin Rapids Sunday[293]
- Sunday guests at the Levi Gonia home were Mrs. Frank Chatfield, son, Clinton, and daughters Gladys, Beulah, and Dorothy, of Oconomowoc and Mr. and Mrs. Hjalmer Olson, and son, Gerald, of Fort Atkinson[294]

Alice Jane Chatfield and Levi R Gonia had three known children:

3.   i.   KATHRYN MABEL GONIA was born 29 Jul 1893 in Troy.[295] She married Hjalmer Nes Olson on 10 Jan 1911 at Heart Prairie Lutheran Church in Whitewater.[296] Hjalmer was born 15 Oct 1888 in Richmond, Walworth County,

---

[291] "Heart Prairie," *The Whitewater Register* (Whitewater, Wisconsin), 7 Nov 1901, p. 8, digital image, *Irvin L. Young Memorial Library Community History Archive* (http://irvinlyoung.advantage-preservation.com/ : accessed 31 Aug 2020).

[292] "Fox Hunting," *The Whitewater Register* (Whitewater, Wisconsin), 19 Jan 1904, p. 5, digital image, *Irvin L. Young Memorial Library Community History Archive* (http://irvinlyoung.advantage-preservation.com/ : accessed 31 Aug 2020).

[293] "In Honor of Frank Rice," *The Whitewater Register* (Whitewater, Wisconsin), 13 Mar 1930, p. 6, digital image, *Irvin L. Young Memorial Library Community History Archive* (http://irvinlyoung.advantage-preservation.com/ : accessed 31 Aug 2020).

[294] "Sunday Guests," *The Whitewater Register* (Whitewater, Wisconsin), 23 Apr 1936, p. 4, digital image, *Irvin L. Young Memorial Library Community History Archive* (http://irvinlyoung.advantage-preservation.com/ : accessed 31 Aug 2020).

[295] Wisconsin Original Certificate of Death (1987), Kathryn Mabel Olson, Department of Health, Madison.

[296] "U. S. Evangelical Lutheran Church of America, Records, 1875-1940," *Ancestry* (https://www.ancestry.com/imageviewer/collections/60722/images/41742_31494 3-00249?pId=10896015 : accessed 12 Jun 2023), database with images, image 77 of 120, Congregational Records > Wisconsin > Whitewater > Heart Prairie Lutheran Church, Marriages, Kathryn M Gonia to Hjalmer N Olson, 10 Jan 1911.

Wisconsin[297] and baptized 25 Nov 1888 in Heart Prairie Lutheran Church in Whitewater.[298] He died 9 Dec 1948 in Madison, Dane County, Wisconsin, and Hjalmer was buried in Hillside Cemetery in Whitewater.[299] Kathryn died 21 Oct 1987 in Geneva, Walworth County, Wisconsin,[300] and she was buried in Hillside Cemetery.[301]

ii. ARTHUR L GONIA was born 11 Jun 1896 in Troy.[302] He died 11 Jun 1897 at 12 o'clock[303] and is buried in Adams Cemetery.[304]

---

[297] Wisconsin Original Certificate of Death (1948), Hjalmer Olson, Department of Health, Madison; Cornelius Olson Bible, *Bibelen eller, Den Hellige Skrift, indeholdende det Gamle og Nye Testamentes canoniske Bøger* (London: Brittiske og Udenlandske Bibelselskabs Bekostning, 1855). The Bible is currently in the possession of Cornelius Olson's great grandson, [(PRIVATE)], Whitewater, Wisconsin.

[298] "U. S. Evangelical Lutheran Church of America, Records, 1875-1940," *Ancestry* (https://www.ancestry.com/imageviewer/collections/60722/images/41742_31494 3-00229?pId=4895856 : accessed 12 Jun 2023), database with images, image 57 of 120, Congregational Records > Wisconsin > Whitewater > Heart Prairie Lutheran Church, Baptisms, Hjalmer Nis Olson, 25 Nov 1888.

[299] Wisconsin Original Certificate of Death (1948), Hjalmer Olson, Department of Health, Madison; and "Hjalmer Olson Dies of Heart Attack," obituary, *The Whitewater Register* (Whitewater, Wisconsin), 16 Dec 1948, p. 1, digital image, *Irvin L. Young Memorial Library Community History Archive* (http://irvinlyoung.advantage-preservation.com/ : accessed 31 Aug 2020).

[300] Wisconsin Original Certificate of Death (1987), Kathryn Mabel Olson, Department of Health, Madison.

[301] *Find A Grave.* Database with images. (http://www.findagrave.com : accessed 22 Aug 2020), memorial 135551660, Kathryn M Gonia Olson (1893-1987), Hillside Cemetery, Whitewater, Walworth County, Wisconsin; gravestone photograph by AGruling.

[302] "Midwife Helped Deliver Over 100 Babies Here!" *The East Troy News*, Wisconsin, 18 Mar 1970.

[303] "Little Arthur L," obituary, *The Whitewater Register* (Whitewater, Wisconsin), 3 Jun 1897, p. 4, digital image, *Irvin L. Young Memorial Library Community History Archive* (http://irvinlyoung.advantage-preservation.com/ : accessed 31 Aug 2020).

[304] *Find A Grave.* Database with images. (http://www.findagrave.com : accessed 21 Aug 2020), memorial 140534706, Arthur L Gonia (1896-1897), Adams Cemetery, Troy, Walworth County, Wisconsin.

iii.   MAUDE GLADYS GONIA was born 13 Jan 1903 in Troy.[305] Gladys married John Rooney on 6 May 1918 in Winnebago County, Illinois.[306] John was born in 1897 in Green Bay, Wisconsin and was a resident of International Falls, Koochiching, Minnesota.[307] Gladys was granted a divorce from John Rooney on 31 May 1921 in International Falls.[308] She married a second time to John Crawford Ralston on 28 Oct 1922 in Fort Atkinson, Jefferson County, Wisconsin.[309] John was born 2 Nov 1892 in Jefferson County, Indiana,[310] died on 19 Aug 1966 in Lafayette, Tippecanoe County, Indiana, and he was buried in Montmorenci Cemetery in Montmorenci, Indiana.[311] She married for a third time to William Earl Barnes on 24 May 1969 in Tippecanoe County, Indiana.[312] Gladys died 15 Aug 1992 in Lafayette, and she was buried in Montmorenci Cemetery in Montmorenci, Indiana.[313]

---

[305] Wisconsin Original Birth Certificate- Delayed (1903), Maude Gladys Gonia, Department of Health, Madison.

[306] "Illinois, County Marriages, 1810-1940," database with images, *FamilySearch* (https://www.familysearch.org : accessed 24 Aug 2020), Maude Gonia to John Rooney, 6 May 1916.

[307] Ibid.

[308] Wisconsin Marriage Certificate (1922), J Crawford Ralston to Mrs. Gladys M Rooney, Department of Health, Madison; Her divorce from John Rooney is cited on her marriage certificate to John Ralston.

[309] Wisconsin Original Birth Certificate- Delayed (1903), Maude Gladys Gonia; Department of Health, Madison. Her marriage is listed in Abstract of Supporting Evidence; Wisconsin Marriage Certificate (1922), J Crawford Ralston to Mrs. Gladys M Rooney, Department of Health, Madison.

[310] "Pioneer in 4-H work, Club Agent Here, Dies," obituary, *The Journal and Courier, Lafayette, Indiana*, 20 Aug 1966, John Crawford Ralston, *Newspapers* (https://www.newspapers.com : accessed 24 Aug 2020).

[311] Indiana Certificate of Death (1966), John Crawford Ralston, Indiana State Board of Health, Indianapolis.

[312] "Indiana, Marriage Certificates, 1960-2005," *Ancestry* (https://www.ancestry.com : accessed 24 Aug 2020), Marriages, Gladys Maude Ralston to William Earl Barnes, 24 May 1969.

[313] Indiana Certificate of Death (1992), Gladys M Barnes, Indiana State Board of Health, Indianapolis.

THIRD GENERATION

3.   KATHRYN MABEL GONIA, the daughter of Alice Jane Chatfield and Levi R Gonia was born 29 Jul 1893 in Troy.[314] She married HJALMER NES OLSON on 10 Jan 1911 at Heart Prairie Lutheran Church in Whitewater.[315] Hjalmer, the son of Cornelius and Anna Katarine Olsen Olson,[316] was born 15 Oct 1888 in Richmond[317] and baptized 25 Nov 1888 in Heart Prairie Lutheran Church in

---

[314] Wisconsin Original Certificate of Death (1987), Kathryn Mabel Olson, Department of Health, Madison; "Mrs. Gonia, 63, of Whitewater, Dies," obituary; "Levi Gonia, 75, Died Here on Wednesday," obituary, *The Whitewater Register*, Wisconsin, 30 Oct 1947, p. 1; Walworth County, Wisconsin Register in Probate, Will and Probate Record for Levi Gonia, No. 21385, vol. 30, p. 48, vol. 225, p. 54, Final Judgment, 17 Jul 1948; 1900 U.S. Census, Walworth County, Wisconsin, population schedule, Troy, p. 8B, Enumeration District 99, Levi R Gonia; database with images, Ancestry (www.ancestry.com : accessed 21 Aug 2020), citing NARA microfilm T623, roll 1821; 1910 U.S. Census, Rock County, Wisconsin, population schedule, Janesville, p. 4A, Enumeration District 120, Levi Gonia; database with images, Ancestry (www.ancestry.com : accessed 24 Aug 2020), citing NARA microfilm T624, roll 1735; 1940 U.S. Census, Walworth County, Wisconsin, population schedule, Whitewater, p. 7A, Enumeration District 32, Levi Gonia; database with images, Ancestry (www.ancestry.com : accessed 24 Aug 2020), citing NARA microfilm T627.
[315] "U. S. Evangelical Lutheran Church of America, Records, 1875-1940," *Ancestry* (https://www.ancestry.com/imageviewer/collections/60722/images/41742_31494 3-00249?pId=10896015 : accessed 12 Jun 2023), database with images, image 77 of 120, Congregational Records > Wisconsin > Whitewater > Heart Prairie Lutheran Church, Marriages, Kathryn M Gonia to Hjalmer N Olson, 10 Jan 1911; The marriage record of Kathryn Mabel Gonia and Hjalmer Nes Olson shows Kathryn's parent's names written in very small handwriting as Lever and Ella Gonia. Other names listed in that church record were also misspelled and crossed out on that page, so it is likely a spelling error, or the person writing down the information misheard the names of Levi and Alice. All other documentation shows the names to be spelled Levi and Alice.
[316] "U. S. Evangelical Lutheran Church of America, Records, 1875-1940," *Ancestry* (https://www.ancestry.com/imageviewer/collections/60722/images/41742_31494 3-00229?pId=4895856 : accessed 12 Jun 2023), database with images, image 57 of 120, Congregational Records > Wisconsin > Whitewater > Heart Prairie Lutheran Church, Baptisms, Hjalmer Nis Olson, 25 Nov 1888.
[317] Wisconsin Original Certificate of Death (1948), Hjalmer Olson, Department of Health, Madison; Cornelius Olson Bible, *Bibelen eller, Den Hellige Skrift, indeholdende det Gamle og Nye Testamentes canoniske Boger* (London: Brittiske og Udenlandske Bibelselskabs Bekostning, 1855).

Whitewater.[318] He died 9 Dec 1948 in Madison, Dane County, Wisconsin.[319] Kathryn died 21 Oct 1987 in Geneva, Walworth County, Wisconsin.[320] She and Hjalmer are buried in Hillside Cemetery in Whitewater.[321].

Biographical Sketch of Kathryn Mabel Gonia and Hjalmer Nes Olson

Kathryn, or Kittie, as she was known by some family and friends,[322] made an early entrance into the world, when the wagon her mother Alice was riding in tipped over and Kathryn was born prematurely weighing only two pounds.[323] According to a 2006 newspaper article, her midwife grandmother, Catherine Chatfield refused to listen to the doctor's grim prognosis about the unlikely survival of a two pound

---

[318] "U. S. Evangelical Lutheran Church of America, Records, 1875-1940," *Ancestry* (https://www.ancestry.com/imageviewer/collections/60722/images/41742_31494 3-00229?pId=4895856 : accessed 12 Jun 2023), database with images, image 57 of 120, Congregational Records > Wisconsin > Whitewater > Heart Prairie Lutheran Church, Baptisms, Hjalmer Nis Olson, 25 Nov 1888.

[319] Wisconsin Original Certificate of Death (1948), Hjalmer Olson, Department of Health, Madison; and and "Hjalmer Olson Dies of Heart Attack," obituary, *The Whitewater Register* (Whitewater, Wisconsin), 16 Dec 1948, p. 1, digital image, *Irvin L. Young Memorial Library Community History Archive* (http://irvinlyoung.advantage-preservation.com/ : accessed 31 Aug 2020).

[320] Wisconsin Original Certificate of Death (1987), Kathryn Mabel Olson, Department of Health, Madison; "Olson, Kathryn M," obituary, *Janesville Daily Gazette*, Wisconsin, 22 Oct 1987, p. 9.

[321] *Find A Grave*. Database with images. (http://www.findagrave.com : accessed 22 Aug 2020), memorial 135551660, Kathryn M Gonia Olson (1893-1987), Hillside Cemetery, Whitewater, Walworth County, Wisconsin; gravestone photograph by AGruling; and Wisconsin Original Certificate of Death (1948), Hjalmer Olson, Department of Health, Madison.

[322] 1900 U.S. Census, Walworth County, Wisconsin, population schedule, Troy, p. 8B, Enumeration District 99, Levi R Gonia; database with images, Ancestry (www.ancestry.com : accessed 21 Aug 2020), citing NARA microfilm T623, roll 1821; and [(PRIVATE)], Whitewater, Wisconsin [(E-ADDRESS FOR PRIVATE USE),] to Julie Schellen, e-mail, 5 September, 2020, "Kittie Gonia Olson," Personal Correspondence Folder, Chatfield Research Files; privately held by Schellen [(E-ADDRESS), & STREET ADDRESS FOR PRIVATE USE], Colleyville, Texas, 2020.

[323] "Midwife Helped Deliver Over 100 Babies Here!" *The East Troy News*, Wisconsin, 18 Mar 1970; and "Remember When," *The Whitewater Register*, Wisconsin, 7 Jun 2012.

baby born in 1893, kept Kathryn in a shoe box in the oven for warmth,[324] and baby Kathryn ended up living a very long life.[325]

Hjalmer Olson
[Courtesy of Karl and Janet Olson]

Kathryn and her parents moved into her grandparent's home on 6 Apr 1897,[326] but by 1900, she and her parents were living with her Aunt Mayme Gonia next door to her grandparents Silas and Catherine Chatfield, where Levi worked as a day laborer.[327] Kathryn's sister Maude was born 13 Jan 1903 and would become Kathryn's first sibling to survive and keep her company at their home.[328] The next year, Kathryn's father Levi began working at the sorghum mill for her grandfather Silas in September 1904,[329] but by the next year Levi, Alice, Kathryn and Maude would be living in La Grange, Walworth County,

[324] "Remember When," *The Whitewater Register*, Wisconsin, 7 Sep 2006, p. 5.

[325] Wisconsin Original Certificate of Death (1987), Kathryn Mabel Olson, Department of Health, Madison.

[326] "It's Not Quite May 1st," *The Whitewater Register* (Whitewater, Wisconsin), 8 Apr 1897, p. 8, digital image, *Irvin L. Young Memorial Library Community History Archive* (http://irvinlyoung.advantage-preservation.com/ : accessed 31 Aug 2020).

[327] 1900 U.S. Census, Walworth County, Wisconsin, population schedule, Troy, p. 8B, Enumeration District 99, Levi R Gonia; database with images, Ancestry (www.ancestry.com : accessed 21 Aug 2020), citing NARA microfilm T623, roll 1821.

[328] Wisconsin Original Birth Certificate- Delayed (1903), Maude Gladys Gonia, Department of Health, Madison.

[329] "Levi Gonia Commenced," *The Whitewater Register* (Whitewater, Wisconsin), 30 Sep 1904, p. 5, digital image, *Irvin L. Young Memorial Library Community History Archive* (http://irvinlyoung.advantage-preservation.com/ : accessed 31 Aug 2020).

Wisconsin, where Levi would be employed as a farm laborer.[330] By 1910, Kathryn was living with her parents and sister Maude in Johnstown, Rock County, Wisconsin where Levi was a farmer.[331] That year, her father Levi appeared to be doing better financially and had employed an extra farm hand, Clair Bice to help on the farm.[332]

Hjalmer Olson, the son of Norwegian immigrant Cornelius Olson and his wife Anna Katarine Olsen,[333] was born 15 Oct 1888 in Richmond, Walworth County, Wisconsin. [334] Hjalmer's mother Anna was born on 10 Oct 1852 in Richmond,[335] and Hjalmer's father, Cornelius was born on 8 Jan 1839 and baptized in Sannidal, Telemark, Norway on 17 Feb

[330] 1905 Wisconsin State Census, Walworth County, La Grange, p. 251, Levi P Gonia; database with images, Ancestry (www.ancestry.com : accessed 24 Aug 2020).

[331] 1910 U.S. Census, Rock County, Wisconsin, population schedule, Johnstown, p. 4A, Enumeration District 120, Levi Gonia; database with images, Ancestry (www.ancestry.com : accessed 24 Aug 2020), citing NARA microfilm T624, roll 1735.

[332] 1910 U.S. Census, Rock County, Wisconsin.

[333] "U. S. Evangelical Lutheran Church of America, Records, 1875-1940," *Ancestry* (https://www.ancestry.com/imageviewer/collections/60722/images/41742_314943-00229?pId=4895856 : accessed 12 Jun 2023), database with images, image 57 of 120, Congregational Records > Wisconsin > Whitewater > Heart Prairie Lutheran Church, Baptisms, Hjalmer Nis Olson, 25 Nov 1888.

[334] Wisconsin Original Certificate of Death (1948), Hjalmer Olson, Department of Health, Madison.

[335] Cornelius Olson Bible, *Bibelen eller, Den Hellige Skrift, indeholdende det Gamle og Nye Testamentes canoniske Bøger* (London: Brittiske og Udenlandske Bibelselskabs Bekostning, 1855); "U. S. Evangelical Lutheran Church of America, Records, 1875-1940," *Ancestry* (https://www.ancestry.com/imageviewer/collections/60722/images/41742_314470-00202?pId=671997 : accessed 11 Jun 2023), database with images, image 145 of 1017, Congregational Records > Wisconsin > Whitewater > First English, Church Burial Record, Anna Cathrina Olson, 6 Apr 1929; Wisconsin Original Certificate of Death (1929), Anna C Olson, Department of Health, Madison. Anna's Wisconsin death certificate shows her birth date to be 23 May 1852, which appears to be a calculation error, since the years, months, days on the same certificate show 76 years, 5 months, and 23 days, which calculates to 14 Oct 1852. The calculated date is still off by four days compared to the Church Burial Record. The Church Burial Record and her husband Cornelius' Bible give her birth date as 10 Oct 1852, which is the date used here.

1839.[336] The town of Sannidal, originally known as Sandøkedal, was a former town in Telemark County which was incorporated into the town of Kragerø in 1960[337]. The town is located at the end of the Kil fiord and was one of the earliest settlements in that part of Norway.[338]

Anna Olson
[Courtesy of Karl and Janet Olson]

Norway is a land of mountains, forests, lakes, glaciers, and fjords. Mountains make up fifty-nine percent of the terrain, and less than five percent of the country's land is suited for agricultural pursuits.[339] In 1835, about ninety percent of Norwegians lived and worked in rural fishing, farming and hunting communities, and survival in the long and cold Norwegian winters required family members young and old to help cultivate the soil and gather food all year.[340]

Farming in Norway was rarely profitable, and for many farmers, it was difficult to make enough money to pay off mortgages much less save

[336] "Norway, Select Baptisms, 1634-1927," database with images, *Ancestry* (https://www.ancestry.com : accessed 9 Sep 2020), Baptisms, Cornelius Olson, birth, 8 Jan 1839, baptism 17 Feb 1839; Cornelius Olson Bible, *Bibelen eller, Den Hellige Skrift, indeholdende det Gamle og Nye Testamentes canoniske Bøger* (London: Brittiske og Udenlandske Bibelselskabs Bekostning, 1855).
[337] *Wikipedia* (http://en.wikipedia.org : accessed 7 Sep 2020), "Sannidal."
[338] Ibid.
[339] George T Flom, *A History of Norwegian Immigration to the United States : From the Earliest Beginning down to the Year 1848* (http:// www.gutenberg.org/files : accessed 7 Sep 2020).
[340] A. Dahlmann, *Norway and its age-old farming culture* (https://talknorway.no/norway-and-its-age-old-farming-culture/ : accessed 7 Sep 2020).

any money.[341] During the mid-nineteenth century, religious persecution, blights, crop failures, poor harvests, and subsequent poverty led a great many Norwegians to search for better economic conditions in the United States.[342]

According to a 2006 *Whitewater Register* newspaper article, Hjalmer's father, Cornelius owned three fishing boats and a farm in Norway, when a terrible storm destroyed his fleet of fishing boats.[343] Shortly thereafter, he emigrated to the United States in 1862.[344] More than a decade later, Cornelius purchased seventy-one and 51/100 acres in Richmond, Walworth County, Wisconsin from N. M. and Catharine Harrington on 21 Apr 1873 for an undisclosed sum.[345] A few years later, Cornelius purchased thirty acres in Richmond from Halvor and May Olson on 10 Apr 1875 for the sum of $800.00.[346] Cornelius went

---

[341] George T Flom, *A History of Norwegian Immigration to the United States : From the Earliest Beginning down to the Year 1848* (http:// www.gutenberg.org/files : accessed 7 Sep 2020).

[342] *Wikipedia* (http://en.wikipedia.org : accessed 7 Sep 2020), "Norwegian Americans."

[343] "Remember When," *The Whitewater Register*, Wisconsin, 7 Sep 2006, p. 5. The newspaper article was written by Marilyn Kienbaum. Although Hjalmer's son Gerald Olson was alive at the time, it is unclear who provided the information to Ms. Kienbaum.

[344] 1900 U.S. Census, Walworth County, Wisconsin, population schedule, Richmond, p. 3, Enumeration District 95, Cornelius Oleson; database with images, Ancestry (www.ancestry.com : accessed 9 Sep 2020), citing NARA microfilm T623, roll 1821.

[345] *FamilySearch* (https://www.familysearch.org/ark:/61903/3:1:3Q9M-C3Q8-MS13-G?i=496&cat=571568 : accessed 12 Jun 2023), digital film, image 497 of 792, "Deeds, 1839-1921; Indexes 1839-1901," Richmond, Walworth County, Wisconsin, vol 59, p. 401, N. M. Harrington and Catharine, his wife of Delavan to Cornelius Oleson of Richmond, signed 21 Apr 1873, recorded 13 Apr 1876.

[346] *FamilySearch* (https://www.familysearch.org/ark:/61903/3:1:3Q9M-C3Q8-MSYG-M?i=497&cat=571568 : accessed 12 Jun 2023), digital film, image 498 of 792, "Deeds, 1839-1921; Indexes 1839-1901," Richmond, Walworth County, Wisconsin, vol 59, p. 402, Halvor Oleson and May, his wife of Richmond to Cornelius Oleson of Richmond, signed 10 Apr 1876, recorded 13 Apr 1876.

to the courthouse and filed both deeds at the same time on 13 Apr 1876.[347]

In 1900, Hjalmer was living in Richmond with his parents, siblings, and grandfather Nes Olson, where Hjalmer's father Cornelius was working as a farmer. A farm hand, Lewis Larson also lived with the family, and Hjalmer was in school and could read and write.[348] Hjalmer's father, Cornelius died 22 May 1902 in Richmond.[349] Cornelius' widow Anna was appointed administratrix of his estate, which named five children, including Hjalmer, and it was finalized on 13 Apr 1903.[350] Cornelius' estate included two hundred and eleven acres of land worth almost $6,000 and personal property worth almost $1200.[351] Hjalmer was still living with his widowed mother Anna and his younger sister Lena, where he was working as a farmer in 1910.[352]

---

347 *FamilySearch* (https://www.familysearch.org/ark:/61903/3:1:3Q9M-C3Q8-MS13-G?i=496&cat=571568 : accessed 12 Jun 2023), digital film, image 497 and 498 of 792, "Deeds, 1839-1921; Indexes 1839-1901," Richmond, Walworth County, Wisconsin, vol 59, p. 401-402, recorded 13 Apr 1876.
348 1900 U.S. Census, Walworth County, Wisconsin, population schedule, Richmond, p. 3, Enumeration District 95, Cornelius Oleson; database with images, *Ancestry* (www.ancestry.com : accessed 9 Sep 2020), citing NARA microfilm T623, roll 1821.
349 Wisconsin Original Certificate of Death (1902), Cornelious Oleson, Department of Health, Madison.
350 "Wisconsin Wills and Probate Records, 1800-1987," Walworth County, *Ancestry* (https://www.ancestry.com/imageviewer/collections/9088/images/007709638_00778?pId=963155 : accessed 12 Jun 2023), database with images, images begin at 778 of 1508, Walworth > Probate Case Files, No 4156-4255, Cornelius Olson, No. 4208, vol 4, p. 366, vol 57, p. 225, Final Judgment, 13 Apr 1903.
351 "Wisconsin Wills and Probate Records, 1800-1987," Walworth County, *Ancestry* (https://www.ancestry.com/imageviewer/collections/9088/images/007709638_00778?pId=963155 : accessed 12 Jun 2023), database with images, images begin at 778 of 1508, Walworth > Probate Case Files, No 4156-4255, Cornelius Olson, No. 4208, vol 4, p. 366, vol 57, p. 225, Final Judgment, 13 Apr 1903.
352 1910 U.S. Census, Walworth County, Wisconsin, population schedule, Richmond, p. 3B, Enumeration District 147, Anna Olson; database with images, *Ancestry* (www.ancestry.com : accessed 13 Sep 2020), citing NARA microfilm T624, roll 1740.

Kathryn Gonia married Hjalmer Olson on 10 Jan 1911 in Whitewater.[353] Whitewater, Wisconsin, located in the Kettle Moraine State Forest, was settled in 1836.[354] A rural community, Whitewater was founded where Whitewater Creek meets Spring Brook, and the town earned its name because of the white sands in its creek beds.[355] Whitewater's population began to grow after the Old Stone Mill was built, and the railway's eventual stop in Whitewater in 1852 spurred its industrial growth.[356]

Kathryn gave birth to their first son, Howard Arthur Olson on 10 Jun 1916,[357] but by the next year Howard became seriously ill with bronchial

Hjalmer and Lena Olson
[Courtesy of Karl and Janet Olson]

[353] "U. S. Evangelical Lutheran Church of America, Records, 1875-1940," *Ancestry* (https://www.ancestry.com/imageviewer/collections/60722/images/41742_314943-00249?pId=10896015 : accessed 12 Jun 2023), database with images, image 77 of 120, Congregational Records > Wisconsin > Whitewater > Heart Prairie Lutheran Church, Marriages, Kathryn M Gonia to Hjalmer N Olson, 10 Jan 1911.

[354] *A Community Rich in History* (https://www.discoverwhitewater.org/tourism-council/history-of-whitewater : accessed 15 Sep 2020).

[355] *Wikipedia* (http://en.wikipedia.org : accessed 15 Sep 2020), "Whitewater, Wisconsin."

[356] *A Community Rich in History* (https://www.discoverwhitewater.org/tourism-council/history-of-whitewater : accessed 15 Sep 2020).

[357] "U. S. Evangelical Lutheran Church of America, Records, 1875-1940," *Ancestry* (https://www.ancestry.com/imageviewer/collections/60722/images/41742_314470-00162?pId=671464 : accessed 12 Jun 2023), database with image, image 105 of 1017, Congregational Records > Wisconsin > Whitewater > First English, Howard Arthur Olson, baptism, 2 Sep 1916.

pneumonia and died on 4 Mar 1917 in Whitewater.[358] Kathryn and Hjalmer were living on Gault Street at the time, and four little girls who had enjoyed pushing Howard's carriage on many occasions, acted as pallbearers during his funeral.[359] Kathryn gave birth to their second son, Russell Eugene Olson on 24 Jun 1919,[360] and the three of them were living with Hjalmer's widowed mother, Anna Olson at 414 South Franklin in Whitewater in January 1920.[361] Russell died less than a year later on 13 Feb 1920.[362]

Hjalmer worked as a foreman at the Whitewater Canning Factory as early as June 1917 and until at least 1923, when they were living at 204 Merchants Avenue in Fort Atkinson, Wisconsin.[363] The Whitewater Canning Factory opened in 1914 and specialized in canned peas, corn,

---

[358] "Howard Arthur Olson," obituary, *The Whitewater Register* (Whitewater, Wisconsin), 9 Mar 1917, p. 1, digital image, *Irvin L. Young Memorial Library Community History Archive* (http://irvinlyoung.advantage-preservation.com/ : accessed 31 Aug 2020).

[359] Ibid.

[360] "U. S. Evangelical Lutheran Church of America, Records, 1875-1940," *Ancestry* (https://www.ancestry.com/imageviewer/collections/60722/images/41742_31447 0-00162?pId=671477 : accessed 12 Jun 2023), database with images, image 105 of 1017, Congregational Records > Wisconsin > Whitewater > First English, Russell Eugene Olson, baptism, 24 Jun 1919.

[361] 1920 U.S. Census, Walworth County, Wisconsin, population schedule, Whitewater, p. 10A, Enumeration District 162, Anna K Olson; database with images, Ancestry (www.ancestry.com : accessed 8 Sep 2020), citing NARA microfilm T625, roll 2019.

[362] *Find A Grave*. Database with images. (http://www.findagrave.com : accessed 27 Aug 2020), memorial 135551783, Russell Eugene Olson (1919-1920), Hillside Cemetery, Whitewater, Walworth County, Wisconsin; gravestone photograph by JBierma.

[363] "U.S., World War I Draft Registration Cards, 1917-1918," Richmond, Walworth County, Wisconsin, *Ancestry* (https://www.ancestry.com : accessed 9 Sep 2020); 1920 U.S. Census, Walworth County, Wisconsin, population schedule, Whitewater, p. 10A, Enumeration District 162, Anna K Olson; database with images, *Ancestry* (www.ancestry.com : accessed 8 Sep 2020); W. D. Hoard and Sons Co, *Fort Atkinson Residential Classified and Rural Directory*, 1923 (http://digital.library.wisc.edu/1711.dl/WI.FADirectory1923 / : accessed 12 Sep 2020), p. 44.

and tomatoes,[364] had the capability of preparing thirty different varieties of peas, and the company's annual payroll in 1916 ran over ten thousand dollars.[365]

The state of Wisconsin became heavily involved in commercial canning in the early twentieth century, as it was an important way to increase the demand for crops and help farmers in the state. During World War I, there was also a strict ration on wheat flour and sugar, and farmers grew additional crops to sell. Families were urged to create home gardens, and canned vegetables became an important staple for many families.[366] By 1920, half of the country's commercially canned

Hjalmer and Kathryn Gonia Olson- 1944
[Courtesy of Karl and Janet Olson]

---

[364] Carol Cartwright, *During Today's Pandemic, Stores are Starting to Limit Meat Purchases Due to Infected Workers at Meat Packing Plants; Were There Food Shortages During the 1918 Influenza Pandemic?* (https://whitewaterbanner.com/food-production-in-1918/ : accessed 9 Sep 2020).

[365] "Whitewater Canning Company," *The Whitewater Register* (Whitewater, Wisconsin), 4 Aug 1916, p. 6, digital image, *Irvin L. Young Memorial Library Community History Archive* (http://irvinlyoung.advantage-preservation.com/ : accessed 9 Sep 2020).

[366] Carol Cartwright, *During Today's Pandemic, Stores are Starting to Limit Meat Purchases Due to Infected Workers at Meat Packing Plants; Were There Food Shortages During the 1918 Influenza Pandemic?* (https://whitewaterbanner.com/food-production-in-1918/ : accessed 9 Sep 2020).

vegetables were produced in Wisconsin.[367] The Whitewater Canning Factory closed in 1962.[368]

Kathryn gave birth to their third son, Gerald Frances Olson on 24 Dec 1924 in Fort Atkinson.[369] Hjalmer, Kathryn and Gerald were living on 514 Roberts Street in Fort Atkinson in 1930, where Hjalmer was employed as a garage mechanic.[370] Hjalmer's mother Anna had been living with her daughter and died the previous year in Whitewater on 6 Apr 1929.[371] Anna was buried in Heart Prairie Cemetery.[372] By 1940 Hjalmer and his family were living with Kathryn's father Levi Gonia on 115 North Prairie in Whitewater, where Hjalmer worked as a repair mechanic.[373] A couple of years later in 1942, Hjalmer can be found working at the Whitewater Garment Company.[374]

[367] "Pass the Peas, Please: Wisconsin's Canning History" 21 Oct 2019 (https://recollectionwisconsin.org/canning : accessed 9 Sep 2020).

[368] Carol Cartwright, *During Today's Pandemic, Stores are Starting to Limit Meat Purchases Due to Infected Workers at Meat Packing Plants; Were There Food Shortages During the 1918 Influenza Pandemic?* (https://whitewaterbanner.com/food-production-in-1918/ : accessed 9 Sep 2020).

[369] Wisconsin Original Certificate of Death (2008), Gerald Francis Olson, Department of Health, Madison.

[370] 1930 U.S. Census, Jefferson County, Wisconsin, population schedule, Fort Atkinson, p. 4B, Enumeration District 12, Hjalmer N Olson; database with images, *Ancestry* (www.ancestry.com : accessed 13 Sep 2020) , citing NARA microfilm T626, roll 2667.

[371] Wisconsin Original Certificate of Death (1929), Anna C Olson, Department of Health, Madison; "Olson," obituary, *The Whitewater Register* (Whitewater, Wisconsin), 11 Apr 1929, p. 8, digital image, *Irvin L. Young Memorial Library Community History Archive* (http://irvinlyoung.advantage-preservation.com/ : accessed 15 Sep 2020).

[372] U. S. Evangelical Lutheran Church of America, Records, 1875-1940," *Ancestry* (https://www.ancestry.com/imageviewer/collections/60722/images/41742_31447 0-00202?pId=671997 : accessed 11 Jun 2023), database with images, image 145 of 1017, Congregational Records > Wisconsin > Whitewater > First English, Church Burial Record, Anna Cathrina Olson, 6 Apr 1929.

[373] 1940 U.S. Census, Walworth County, Wisconsin, population schedule, Whitewater, p. 7A, Enumeration District 32, Levi Gonia; database with images, *Ancestry* (www.ancestry.com : accessed 24 Aug 2020) , citing NARA microfilm T627, roll 4643.

[374] "U.S., World War II Draft Registration Cards, 1942," Whitewater, Walworth County, Wisconsin, *Ancestry* (https://www.ancestry.com : accessed 14 Sep 2020).

The Whitewater Garment Company, founded by Leo Perry and originally known as the Kinzie Rubber Manufacturing Company, was the first and at one point the largest raincoat manufacturer in the Midwest.[375] During World War II, Whitewater Garment Company provided employment to around four-hundred and fifty people in and around the Whitewater area.[376]

In July 1946, Hjalmer Olson's address was still at 115 North Prairie in Whitewater,[377] and his final employer would be General Motors in Janesville.[378] General Motors purchased the Samson Tractor Company in Janesville in 1918 in order to begin selling farm vehicles.[379] The first tractor was produced on 1 May 1919, and cars were added to the Janesville production line in 1923.[380] By 1942, General Motors temporarily ceased production of vehicles to manufacture 105mm artillery shells as part of the World War II war effort.[381] The General Motors plant in Janesville closed in 2009.[382]

---

[375] Fred G. Kraege, *Whitewater*, (Mount Pleasant, South Carolina : Arcadia Publishing, 2006).

[376] Ibid.

[377] Wisconsin Telephone Company. *Whitewater Telephone Directory, including Lima Center.* (Madison, Wisconsin : July 1946), p. 31.

[378] "Hjalmer Olson Dies of Heart Attack," obituary, *The Whitewater Register* (Whitewater, Wisconsin), 16 Dec 1948, p. 1, digital image, *Irvin L. Young Memorial Library Community History Archive* (http://irvinlyoung.advantage-preservation.com/ : accessed 31 Aug 2020).

[379] *Wisconsin Historical Society*, "General Motors Plant, Janesville" (https://www.wisconsinhistory.org/Records/Article/CS2419/ : accessed 18 Sep 2020).

[380] *Wikipedia* (http://en.wikipedia.org : accessed 18 Sep 2020), "Janesville Assembly Plant."

[381] *Wisconsin Historical Society*, "General Motors Plant, Janesville" (https://www.wisconsinhistory.org/Records/Article/CS2419/ : accessed 18 Sep 2020).

[382] *Wikipedia* (http://en.wikipedia.org : accessed 18 Sep 2020), "Janesville Assembly Plant."

Hjalmer Olson died on 9 Dec 1948 at the Methodist Hospital in Madison, Dane County, Wisconsin.[383] When Hjalmer died, he was still living in the home that his father-in-law Levi Gonia purchased in 1928 at 115 North Prairie in Whitewater.[384] Hjalmer's widow, Kathryn still resided there in December 1950,[385] but by 1959 she had moved down the street to 179 North Prairie[386] next door to her son Gerald Olson and his family who moved to 203 North Prairie in 1957.[387]

Kathryn was still living at the same address in 1976,[388] but when she became unable to live alone, she moved to an assisted living facility.[389] She was so popular with the staff that the female employees took their breaks in Kathryn's room just to talk with her.[390] She outlived Hjalmer

---

[383] Wisconsin Original Certificate of Death (1948), Hjalmer Olson, Department of Health, Madison; and "Hjalmer Olson Dies of Heart Attack," obituary, *The Whitewater Register* (Whitewater, Wisconsin), 16 Dec 1948, p. 1, digital image, *Irvin L. Young Memorial Library Community History Archive* (http://irvinlyoung.advantage-preservation.com/ : accessed 31 Aug 2020). Neither the Walworth County, Wisconsin Register in Probate or Dane County Clerk of Courts/Probate/Records Department could locate the probate record of Hjalmer Olson.

[384] Wisconsin Original Certificate of Death (1948), Hjalmer Olson, Department of Health, Madison.

[385] Wisconsin Telephone Company. *Whitewater Telephone Directory, including Lima Center.* (Madison, Wisconsin : Dec 1950), p. 13.

[386] "Just Right for Mom," *The Whitewater Register* (Whitewater, Wisconsin), 30 Apr 1959, p. 6, digital image, *Irvin L. Young Memorial Library Community History Archive* (http://irvinlyoung.advantage-preservation.com/ : accessed 17 Sep 2020). A search was made in the Walworth County, Wisconsin, Deed Records for the sale of the 115 North Prairie property and the purchase of the 179 North Prairie property, but neither of the deed records could be located by the Walworth County Register of Deeds.

[387] Walworth County, Wisconsin, Deed Records, vol. 518, p. 38, No. P494654, Earl and Barbara E. Tannenbaum, his wife to Gerald F. Olson and Jean I. Olson, his wife, recorded 18 Oct 1957; "City of Whitewater Residential Property Assessment Roll, 1960," *The Whitewater Register* (Whitewater, Wisconsin), 8 Sep 1960, p. 18, digital image, *Irvin L. Young Memorial Library Community History Archive* (http://irvinlyoung.advantage-preservation.com/ : accessed 17 Sep 2020).

[388] "Police Report," *The Whitewater Register*, Wisconsin, 4 Mar 1976, p. 3 (http://irvinlyoung.advantage-preservation.com/ : accessed 17 Sep 2020).

[389] "Remember When," *The Whitewater Register* (Whitewater, Wisconsin), 7 Sep 2006, p. 5.

[390] Ibid.

by almost thirty-nine years,[391] and Kathryn died at the Lakeland Nursing Home in Geneva, Walworth County, Wisconsin on 21 Oct 1987.[392] She and Hjalmer are buried in Hillside Cemetery in Whitewater.[393]

Kathryn signed her will fourteen years before her death on 3 Apr 1973, and after her debts were paid, she left the remainder of her estate to her son, Gerald F. Olson, who was living in Milton, Wisconsin at the time.[394] In the Final Distribution of the Estate on 3 Jun 1988, Gerald received $29,452.28, including the property on 179 North Prairie, which was appraised at $33,365.07.[395]

Kathryn "Kittie" Gonia
[Courtesy of East Troy Area Historical Society]

Kathryn Mabel Gonia and husband, Hjalmer Nes Olson enjoyed an active social life and volunteered at community events. A few newspaper excerpts include:

---

[391] "Olson, Kathryn M," obituary, *Janesville Daily Gazette*, Wisconsin, 22 Oct 1987, p. 9.

[392] Wisconsin Original Certificate of Death (1987), Kathryn Mabel Olson, Department of Health, Madison.

[393] *Find A Grave*. Database with images. (http://www.findagrave.com : accessed 22 Aug 2020), memorial 135551660, Kathryn M Gonia Olson (1893-1987), Hillside Cemetery, Whitewater, Walworth County, Wisconsin; gravestone photograph by AGruling; and Wisconsin Original Certificate of Death (1948), Hjalmer Olson, Department of Health, Madison.

[394] Walworth County, Wisconsin Register in Probate, Will and Probate Record for Kathryn Olson, File No. 87 PR 423, vol. 436, p. 245, Will signed 3 Apr 1973 and recorded 5 Nov 1987.

[395] Walworth County, Wisconsin Register in Probate, Will and Probate Record for Kathryn Olson, Final Distribution, dated 3 Jun 1988.

- Mr. and Mrs. Levi Gonia entertained Mr. and Mrs. H. N. Olson and son Gerald of Fort Atkinson and Alfred Thompson of Elkhorn Friday evening in honor of Mr. and Mrs. J. C. Ralston and family.[396]

- ...according to [the Whitewater Chapter of the Red Cross] War Fund Chairman Avis Cleland, the following men and women will make house-to-house calls [asking for money] with others yet unassigned on various neighborhoods...Mrs. Hjalmer Olson, east side of North Prairie...[397]

- Mr. and Mrs. Hjalmer Olson had as their guests last week from Wednesday until Saturday their nieces, the Misses Ruth and Marjorie Ralston of Lafayette, Indiana. The latter Miss Ralston recently graduated from Purdue University located at Lafayette.[398]

- ...During the next two weeks the Ladies Aid will be soliciting funds... for the new building at Homme Orphan's Home, at Wittenburg, Wisconsin... The committee consists of...Mrs. Hjalmer Olson...[399]

- At the annual business meeting of First English Lutheran Church of this city held Monday evening, Harvey Larson was elected to the Board of Trustees... Mrs. Hjalmer Olson to the board of Deaconess of Sunshine Committee...[400]

- Mr. and Mrs. Hjalmer Olson, their son and daughter-in-law, Mr. and Mrs. Gerald Olson, and the latter's small daughter,

---

[396] "Mr. and Mrs. J. C. Ralston," *The Whitewater Register* (Whitewater, Wisconsin), 13 Mar 1930, p. 6, digital image, *Irvin L. Young Memorial Library Community History Archive* (http://irvinlyoung.advantage-preservation.com/ : accessed 31 Aug 2020).

[397] "Our Number One Job at the Moment- Dig for the Red Cross," *The Whitewater Register* (Whitewater, Wisconsin), 2 Mar 1944, p. 1, digital image, *Irvin L. Young Memorial Library Community History Archive* (http://irvinlyoung.advantage-preservation.com/ : accessed 9 Sep 2020).

[398] "Ruth and Marjorie Ralston," *The Whitewater Register* (Whitewater, Wisconsin), 9 Mar 1944, p. 4, digital image, *Irvin L. Young Memorial Library Community History Archive* (http://irvinlyoung.advantage-preservation.com/ : accessed 31 Aug 2020).

[399] "Homme Orphan's Home," *The Whitewater Register* (Whitewater, Wisconsin), 19 Oct 1944, p. 3, digital image, *Irvin L. Young Memorial Library Community History Archive* (http://irvinlyoung.advantage-preservation.com/ : accessed 31 Aug 2020).

[400] "First Lutheran Holds its Annual Business Meeting," *The Whitewater Register* (Whitewater, Wisconsin), 11 Jan 1945, p. 1, digital image, *Irvin L. Young Memorial Library Community History Archive* (http://irvinlyoung.advantage-preservation.com/ : accessed 31 Aug 2020).

Margery Kristine, attended the 100th year celebration Sunday at the Chatfield farm, that has been in the senior Mrs. Olson's mother's family for more than a century... Mrs. Olson wore her grandmother's silk skirt, 91 years old to the celebration.[401]

- The Eli Pierce chapter of the D.A.R. approved schools, at 2 p.m. Wednesday in Bassett House... Among interesting features of the afternoon will be a display of rare old glassware and Majorca ware shown by Mrs. Hjalmer Olson.[402]
- ...The Ladies Aid Society of First English Lutheran Church will meet at 8 p.m. Tuesday in Fellowship Hall. Mmes Alfred Thompson, Ben Olson, and Hjalmer Olson are co-hostesses.[403]

Kathryn Mabel Gonia and Hjalmer Nes Olson had three known children:

    i.   HOWARD ARTHUR OLSON was born 10 Jun 1916 and baptized 2 Sep 1916 in Whitewater.[404] He died on 4 Mar 1917 after suffering from bronchial pneumonia for several

---

[401] "Whitewater Briefs," *Janesville Daily Gazette* (Whitewater, Wisconsin), Tuesday, 20 Jul 1948, p. 9, digital image, *Irvin L. Young Memorial Library Community History Archive* (http://www.newspapers.com/ : accessed 26 Sep 2020).

[402] "Rare Old Glassware," *Janesville Daily Gazette* (Whitewater, Wisconsin), Monday, 15 Nov 1948, p. 12, digital image, *Irvin L. Young Memorial Library Community History Archive* (http://www.newspapers.com/ : accessed 4 Apr 2019).

[403] "Ladies Aid Society," *The Whitewater Register* (Whitewater, Wisconsin), 27 Sep 1951, p. 4, digital image, *Irvin L. Young Memorial Library Community History Archive* (http://irvinlyoung.advantage-preservation.com/ : accessed 31 Aug 2020).

[404] "U. S. Evangelical Lutheran Church of America, Records, 1875-1940," *Ancestry* (https://www.ancestry.com/imageviewer/collections/60722/images/41742_31447 0-00162?pId=671464 : accessed 12 Jun 2023), database with images, image 105 of 1017, Congregational Records > Wisconsin > Whitewater > First English, Howard Arthur Olson, baptism, 2 Sep 1916.

days.[405] He was buried 6 Mar 1917 [406] in Hillside Cemetery in Whitewater.[407]

ii.   RUSSELL EUGENE OLSON was born 24 Jun 1919 and baptized 21 Sep 1919 in Whitewater.[408] He died 13 Feb 1920 and is buried in Hillside Cemetery.[409]

iii.   GERALD FRANCES OLSON was born 24 Dec 1924 in Fort Atkinson, Wisconsin, and he married Jean Broman on 31 Dec 1946 in Whitewater. [410] Gerald "Jerry" served as a

Hjalmer Olson with son, Gerald
[Courtesy of Karl and Janet Olson]

---

[405] "Howard Arthur Olson," obituary, *The Whitewater Register* (Whitewater, Wisconsin), 9 Mar 1917, p. 1, digital image, *Irvin L. Young Memorial Library Community History Archive* (http://irvinlyoung.advantage-preservation.com/ : accessed 31 Aug 2020).

[406] "U. S. Evangelical Lutheran Church of America, Records, 1875-1940," *Ancestry* (https://www.ancestry.com/imageviewer/collections/60722/images/41742_31447 0-00201?pId=671952 : accessed 12 Jun 2023), database with images, image 114 of 1017, Congregational Records > Wisconsin > Whitewater > First English, Burial Record, Howard Arthur Olson, 4 Mar 1917.

[407] *Find A Grave.* Database with images. (http://www.findagrave.com : accessed 27 Aug 2020), memorial 135551530, Howard Arthur Olson (1916-1917), Hillside Cemetery, Whitewater, Walworth County, Wisconsin; gravestone photograph by JBierma.

[408] "U. S. Evangelical Lutheran Church of America, Records, 1875-1940," *Ancestry* (https://www.ancestry.com/imageviewer/collections/60722/images/41742_31447 0-00162?pId=671477 : accessed 12 Jun 2023), database with images, image 105 of 1017, Congregational Records > Wisconsin > Whitewater > First English, Russell Eugene Olson, baptism, 24 Jun 1919.

[409] *Find A Grave.* Database with images. (http://www.findagrave.com : accessed 27 Aug 2020), memorial 135551783, Russell Eugene Olson (1919-1920), Hillside Cemetery, Whitewater, Walworth County, Wisconsin; gravestone photograph by JBierma.

[410] "Gerald F Olson," obituary, *Janesville Gazette*, 5 Apr 2008, *NewspaperArchive* (https://www.newspaperarchive.com : accessed 27 Aug 2020).

Merchant Marine during World War II where he was awarded two purple hearts.[411] He worked as a sales

Gerald Olson, February 1943
[Courtesy of Karl and Janet Olson]

manager at Whitewater Manufacturing for forty-two years.[412] His wife, Jean was involved in an auto accident and died of her injuries on 23 Nov 1977 at Fort Atkinson Memorial Hospital.[413] She is buried in Wisconsin Memorial Park in Brookfield, Wisconsin.[414] Jerry died on 3 Apr 2008 in Elkhorn, Walworth County, Wisconsin and is buried in Wisconsin Memorial Park in Brookfield.[415]

[411] "Gerald F Olson," obituary.

[412] "Remember When," *The Whitewater Register*, Wisconsin, 7 Sep 2006, p. 5; and "Gerald F Olson," obituary, *Janesville Gazette*, 5 Apr 2008, *NewspaperArchive* (https://www.newspaperarchive.com : accessed 27 Aug 2020).

[413] "Accidents Kill Two in Jefferson County," obituary, *Janesville Gazette*, Fri, 25 Nov 1977, Jean I Olson, *NewspaperArchive* (https://www.newspaperarchive.com : accessed 27 Aug 2020).

[414] *Find A Grave*. Database with images. (http://www.findagrave.com : accessed 27 Aug 2020), memorial 187125286, Jean Irene Broman Olson (1926-1977), Hillside Cemetery, Whitewater, Walworth County.

[415] Wisconsin Original Certificate of Death (2008), Gerald Francis Olson, Department of Health, Madison.

www.ingramcontent.com/pod-product-compliance
Lightning Source LLC
Chambersburg PA
CBHW060353130626
46553CB00003B/1203